Praise for Jonathan Johnson

"Johnson is a generous pathologist of the human heart who is careful to leave its mystery intact."

—Lucia Perillo, author of *Time Will Clean the Carcass Bones*

"[In Johnson's work] you find yourself in a world rich in texture, raw with meaning . . . addressed by a voice you learn to trust."

—Adrienne Rich, author of *Of Woman Born: Motherhood as Experience and Institution*

"[Johnson's work is] written with great intensity and skill, and not for the faint of heart but for those who can accept the full burden of consciousness."

—Jim Harrison, author of *Legends of the Fall*

"A moving memoir of how far some will go to hold on to a dream without sacrificing their values."

—Katharine Mieszkowski, *Los Angeles Times*

"Elegant writing and sharp dialogue."

—*Booklist*

"Jonathan Johnson steps across the landscape of relationships that connect us and meditates on the gift of life's small moments."

—Dorianne Laux, author of *Only as the Day Is Long: New and Selected Poems*

"The recovery and discovery of the poet's home place and original people informs these well-wrought poems. Fellow pilgrims will find in Johnson's explorations worthy guidance for their own journeys."

—Thomas Lynch, author of *The Sin Eater: A Breviary*

The Desk on the Sea

The Desk on the Sea

A Memoir by

Jonathan Johnson

Wayne State University Press
Detroit

ISBN 978-0-8143-4665-5 (paperback)
ISBN 978-0-8143-4666-2 (e-book)

Library of Congress Control Number: 2019931682

Publication of this book was made possible by a generous gift from The Meijer Foundation. This work is supported in part by an award from the Michigan Council for Arts and Cultural Affairs.

Wayne State University Press
Leonard N. Simons Building
4809 Woodward Avenue
Detroit, Michigan 48201-1309

Visit us online at wsupress.wayne.edu

Were it not for the way you taught me to look
at the world, to see the life at play in everything,
I would have to be lonely forever.

"Mother," Ted Kooser

Prologue

The mountains or the sea? I'd come to Scotland to answer that question. Though I was alone, the answer I sought wasn't just for myself but for all three of us, my family. The choice loomed large in my mind, like the sea and mountains themselves. Daydreams of the country's landscape and us in it had sustained me through the most difficult period of my life. Now I was finally there, scouting in advance of our move for a year, a year in which I planned to find . . . what? Freedom? A new beginning? My best self? I didn't know. I only knew to look in Scotland. My imagination had been claimed and revived by a mysterious yearning, a compulsion even, to live there. But where exactly? And where would my wife, Amy, and our daughter, Anya, find whatever they might be seeking? This was going to be their year too, and they had trusted me to choose for them.

At the Edinburgh airport, the economy car I'd reserved was sold out.

"But you'll be happy enough," the purple-haired, skinny young man behind the counter told me as he typed and looked at his screen. And sure enough, the replacement car was exquisite. A black Saab 90 with fifteen miles on the odometer. I'd never driven anything so lavish. Even if we could have afforded it—which we most certainly couldn't—I would never have spent the extra for such a luxury; we'd scrupulously squirreled away every dollar we could spare for the coming year. It was my first bit of luck in Scotland. It gave me hope for more to come.

The car drove like an arrow through long and tight parabolas of narrow roads as I followed a Michelin map the size of a bedsheet on the seat beside me from one village circled in red marker to the next. For months that map had been tacked up on our dining room wall back home. Whenever our online search had led us to a cottage that seemed a likely candidate—something in a small village with a little school and trails leading out across the landscape—Amy and I had let Anya, who was almost eight, draw a red circle.

In my first daydreams of Scotland, I had imagined us in the Highlands. Among steep glens and summits where the sheep were specks high on the slopes into which we would hike. Anya had needed to reach up to circle the northern villages on our map.

But those mountainous places were remote, Amy had reminded me. We wouldn't get to know the country's bigger cities and towns much. And most of the Highland villages where we found cottages to let were on lochs, not the coast.

Amy's a native coastal dweller. Home for her has always meant the craggy shore and cove beaches around Marquette, her little upper Michigan city. There, Lake Superior is like a freshwater sea, the world's largest, stretching to the northern horizon, across which the gold lights of iron-ore ships pass at night. Waves boom up against the cliffs in the fall, sending spray into the forest, glazing the branches with ice. Marquette is also where my parents settled and I spent the latter years of my own childhood. It's where Amy and I spoke our wedding vows, in a cliff-top meadow above Superior.

A Scottish friend in America had said that if we liked coastline we should check out the string of little fishing villages south of St. Andrews. Online we found a couple of fishermen's cottages there that we liked. Some had windows from which you could watch sunrise over the North Sea. Anya drew more red circles, these down and to the right on the map, closer to her eye level.

To save money, we decided I'd make the scouting journey alone. I had a few days in May to find us the place into which we'd move in July. I brought a picture Anya had drawn: a little house with a door and two windows, three arched and snow-capped mountains behind, a straight line for the beach, and a squiggly line for waves in front. In big block letters I read each night when I put the drawing on whatever nightstand I'd be sleeping beside, she'd written, "Good by Dady!! I love you!! Git a good house!!"

So, the mountains or the sea?

The question had seemed so important at the time. Which reality would we give ourselves to step into and make a life for a while? I drove that black Saab fast—by American, if not Scottish, standards—between appointments with landlords. Each village we had imagined came into view. The mountains were higher and darker, the sea vaster.

But there was another question pushing me on, I now realize. A question I had yet to articulate to myself.

Was I moving to Scotland to mourn or rejoice?

In the four years since the death of my mother, sorrow had become for me a daily way of life. The world had been empty of the one person I believed knew it best. Knew *me* best. Everything she'd ever thought and seen and felt, every bit of wisdom, every memory in every neuron in that vast galaxy of neurons of her was gone. Nowhere. A few ashes in Lake Superior. Sinking. Floating out.

And yet, through those same four years, she'd been everywhere. In the overflying geese I addressed with "Hi, Mom." In the bright anticipation on faces here and there in each new poetry class I taught. Most of all in my family. In the husband I wanted to be for Amy. In the parent I wanted—more than I'd ever wanted anything—to be for Anya. My mother continued filling me with capacity and gratitude. I could hear her voice. *Look, notice, love.*

It was a false choice, of course, grief or wonder. Even before my mom died, when I knew it was coming, I had understood intellectually that grief and wonder must go on together, the twin poles of what would be my new motherless existence as my mother's son.

But how? Parents die. It's the natural order of things. I was desolate, but for four years I endured, as people do. I had my work, writing and teaching. I had a house, bills, e-mails. I had my new obsession, Scotland, getting closer. All the while, though, sorrow and joy were at war, each determined to claim me, to be the one truth of my existence. The person who had given me my life and taught me to live it was gone. No. She was giving me my life still, still teaching me to live it. No. She, the person herself, was no more. And so on the battles went, through the days into years.

I wept alone in the car a lot. I sang with the windows down.

I knew that the reconciliation of life and death, of grief and wonder, is the great story of the human spirit. I knew it from John Keats and Mozart, both of whom my mother had given me. I knew it from my mother herself. But I couldn't *feel* it. Not in the way I would need to feel it if I were going to pass on to my own child my mother's grace for living in that great paradox.

Maybe in Scotland I could learn. Scotland would be away from the normalcy that had merely sustained me, my job and house and e-mails. And though I had not yet understood why, the beauty and truth of the Scotland I sought—whether in the mountains or beside the sea—would be inseparably somber *and* ecstatic.

Like the life for which I was also looking.

Patients who have been on dialysis for at least six months and who decide to stop dialysis generally live an average of ten days.

Dr. Leslie Spry, National Kidney Foundation

Marquette, Day One

February 2 . . .

"I saw the geese," my mother said. "I think I saw the geese."

Earlier, I talked on the phone with Kosinski. He said he's seen a lot of bad shit, but he's never seen a patient suffer more. His gut says it's over. We're in uncharted territory. He's done hundreds of legs and three or four hands, but never both hands.

He said he'd do it. Go home after and have dinner and go to bed. But is it something we ought to do? He's seen her slide these last weeks. She was always headed this way.

"I tried to let you know that somewhat when you were talking about giving her your kidney. The question even then was how much would you be giving?"

Kosinski also said my mother never would have seen Anya born if not for my dad.

Earlier, when my dad was leaving to teach, my mom, drowsy with ache and morphine, said, "There goes the One and Only. Always, always!"

When we visited at Christmas, I cut a tree for the house.

She was having difficulty eating; her remaining fingers were paining her. Amy helped, and my mom said she was grateful. She said she was grateful "to have people who love me and are so patient with me."

She said, "I should build a monument to your father in the front yard for all he does."

After she found out about her hands, that they couldn't be saved, my mother sat in front of her kitchen window and said, "I saw the geese. I think I saw the geese."

It was snowing heavily outside. It was the depth of winter.

Four years later . . .

Scotland, Midsummer

Amy and Anya and I have found a little patch of sand on an otherwise rocky stretch of coast beside a ruined cottage. The sand is damp from this morning's shower, but it's warm under the afternoon sun. As an eight-year-old, Anya lives about half of her waking life in her imagination. Her interactions with Amy and me are often in character as Harry Potter. Amy is Hermione, and I'm Ron Weasley. About half the time our family goes through the world as these three young friends out for a grand adventure.

Today, the trio is shipwrecked. Our protagonist Harry—the little girl with long blond hair and scarless skin on her forehead—is fixing something to eat, which delights Ron, who is perpetually hungry. Anya digs a little bowl in the sand into which she drops the kelp she collects.

"But Ron doesn't know yet, Daddy."

"He's just hungry for lunch?"

"Right. And Harry's fixing it for him."

The breeze off the North Sea is cool. It moves through our hair and up the grass and through the thistles and empty windows and absent roof of the ruined cottage.

Anya walks out onto the rocks. She is confident on her bare feet. Her cuffs are rolled and dry. I curl my toes in the damp, warm sand. Amy sits beside me, turning the lens of her camera and taking pictures.

The camera gives a little click with each image, and I can see what Amy sees: Anya lifting her arms out to her sides for balance and looking down to search for that next deliciously slimy, long strand of kelp for Ron's castaway soup; Anya hopping off the rocks and back on the sand, her gold hair lifted with her descent, a few strands blown across her face.

"I'm 'ungry, Harry."

"Honestly, Ronald," Hermione chimes in, "Harry's fixing us something as fast as he can." Amy makes a good Hermione. Same curly, dark hair. The same pleasure in feigning exasperation and eye-rolling aloofness over her loyalty and deep affection.

"Beef stew, Harry?" I ask. "With sausages, I hope?"

Anya smiles in spite of herself. "Just wait, Ron."

She mixes the kelp and sand around a bit, carries it back to the rock, and lays it out in three piles.

"OK, it's ready."

Amy lifts the kelp to her chin.

"Mmm . . . thanks, Harry."

"What the bloody Hell is this, Harry?" I demand.

"Lunch, Ron."

"I'd rather starve."

"You could have a cow pie?" Five cows graze just upshore from the ruined cottage. "And, Daddy, Ron only hears the word pie, OK?"

"Pie! Wonderful, Harry!"

Our cottage is in the village around the point a half mile down the shore. We moved in six days ago. For a year Anya will go to school and search the rock pools at low tide for shells and little creatures and likely develop something of a real Scottish accent. Amy will take photos and shop with delight at the village greengrocer and cook slow meals. I'll write poems upstairs in our bedroom at the dropleaf table we've put against the windows. When a ship passes, if I happen to glance up and notice, I'll look in the little telescope to see if I can spot the flag.

We will live a story of our own invention.

But it will be a story without the audience to whom it would have meant the most.

Beside the telescope on the polished, worn wood table is a porcelain creamer I use as a vase for a single thistle and one seagull feather. These I found on the point two or three evenings ago. We'd settled in and finished unpacking, and I'd left for my first walk by myself. In my pocket was one of two tiny green pebbles I'd brought from the cove on Lake Superior where we'd scattered my mother's ashes. I had in mind to place the pebble on the water's edge, where the waves break, so that in bed at night I could imagine I heard my mother's voice in the breath of the surf.

Instead I picked the thistle, took the feather from where it lay beside the grassy path. So the pebble sits there when I write along with its twin, the one I brought to set beside a certain narrow Highland loch from which mountain slopes rise steep on both sides. I'd seen Loch Shiel on a map, pronounced the same as my mother's name, Sheila, just one vowel shorter. She never got to Scotland, and I don't yet know if any of her people, the MacLures, were from the Highlands. But that long narrow loch is where the other pebble from her Lake Superior cove, her grave, will go. If I ever let it go.

Meanwhile they are good company, the two little stones. They are nothing like the bright emerald of my mother's eyes, but they remind me to think of that green. And then I'm recalling her freckled face exactly. The face of the one whose love followed me wherever I went.

And then I am without her again. A son who has lost his mother.

It's become clear to Ron that the pies are not what he'd had in mind, so he's back at his pile of seaweed.

"All right, Harry, here goes," Ron gulps and makes his pained, apprehensive face. I hold the kelp up to my mouth, bend over and make deep hurling sounds. Then I'm on my hands and knees, retching and coughing. I know the exact curve of Anya's smile without looking up.

I couldn't tell you how many amputations my mother had, toes and then toes and then foot, shin, and more shin bone, more toes, and fingers, knuckle to knuckle to nothing, the other foot, thumb. I've lost count. Through all this her surgeon, Dr. Kosinski, became her friend, and in turn a family friend, just Kosinski—the way you'd call an old trouble-maker buddy by his last name. At her funeral, which was a kind of wake at my parents' house, he stood with a drink in his hand and said, for the second time, that he'd never seen anyone suffer as she'd suffered. Kosinski wasn't a young man. He'd had maybe thirty years of practice by that night. I can't imagine what he'd seen, what torments he'd witnessed to compare to hers.

Her final choice had been between losing her hands, what was left of them, and bringing it all to an end, the kidney dialysis, the frostbite-like scalding and blackening of her remaining fingers, the open sore where her left leg ended just below the knee, the narcotic nausea. She had endured years of all this and worse because she wanted to be here, because she loved us and loved every day. Because she could sit at the kitchen table and wave good-bye with both hands as her loved ones backed out the driveway and into the wider world.

"I have a *good* life," my mother said many times over the years, planting her emphasis on "good" so deep and solid in my memory I can hear her clearly now. "A *good* life," with an emphasis that spoke of a satisfied heart. "We don't get the days back," she also used to say.

When she still had one leg she sat in the sun in her wheelchair. Anya, who was then about two, sat in her lap, and my mother pushed them backward with her remaining foot up a ramp I'd recently built to go from the backyard up to the deck. At the top she told Anya to hold on, lifted the foot, and with her only grandchild raised her arms and exclaimed, "Whee!" all the way as they rode to the bottom.

My mother made Amy, sitting in the grass watching, promise not to tell my father. It was a shallow ramp and not long, but my father was the watcher and nurse of my mother's open wounds, the one who would have no doubt imagined most vividly what a fall could mean.

Anya craned her head around to look my mom in the face and declared, "Again, Nana!" And my mom leaned to touch her forehead to my daughter's and called her "my Little Sprite" and agreed to one more and backed them up the ramp again.

Amy kept her promise not to tell my father—until my mother's funeral, when she told the story to the smiles and laughs of everyone crowded into my parents' living room, including my father.

"She made the right choice," Kosinski was saying to me a short time later as he swished the ice in his drink. He repeated more of what he'd told me on the phone before she'd died. "I'd have cut off her hands, gone home, had dinner and a drink, and gone to bed." Blue eyed and burly, fair skinned as my mom, Kosinski has a gift for bluntness, one of the things my mom—diplomatic though she was herself—liked about him. "But it wouldn't have been any good." He shook his head. "The shock and pain would have been worse than with her feet. She didn't have anything left to go through that. If she'd have survived a few months, I'd have been surprised."

Of her cluster of diseases, all that's worth saying is they were the kinds of things people get—some old heart damage, a treated liver disorder, diabetes combined with a not-uncommon small-vessel-and-nerve condition called Raynaud's, and a related autoimmune condition called CREST scleroderma—nothing particularly exotic, no key words of dread. But together the diabetes,

Raynaud's, and scleroderma slowly took her extremities after years of allowing in occasional infections, the antibiotics from which finally destroyed her kidneys. When her palms and the few remaining nubs of her fingers turned purple and white and black, and Kosinski said all that was left to do was take everything to just below both elbows, and he admitted there wasn't much chance she'd outlast the operation by long, and the thrush in her mouth made it painful to talk, and the sores on her back and tailbone were raw to the flesh, and she was buried down under so many narcotics that it took great effort to climb to the surface and open her eyes and smile and say hello, she let go.

There was so much to let go. While her body was being periodically carved away and more and more hours of her days were spent on the business of surviving, her life had kept growing. Movies, cappuccino with my father in the parked car overlooking Lake Superior, her peonies and daylilies blooming (in the last few years when this or that finger was withered and bandaged and she could no longer dig in the dirt, I dug for her while she sat in her chair and supervised), and so much of Anya. Anya—her Little Sprite—running naked out into the backyard. Anya propped up in bed beside her in the morning, both of them drinking from cups with spill-proof lids and big handles. And in February four years ago, on one of those few days my mother was told she'd have left to live when she stopped going to dialysis, Anya turning. Her arms stretched above her head. Turning her pirouette from dance class for my mother, who raised her head and lifted the unimaginable weight of her eyelids to see.

But the hardest thing for my mother about losing my daughter, I would guess, wasn't the reality of never seeing her again, impossibly hard as that must have been—that bright little face fading away with everything else. From what I know of my mother, what was hardest about losing Anya was that there would be no more days to teach her.

Some of how Anya will feel about her life has, I suppose, been settled at eight years old. But much of the quality of her relationship to her life still remains an open question, I know. As her father I also know there's only so much I can do to affect what comes her way in that life. I'll take her to beautiful places like this Scottish coast. I'll teach her to be good to her body and spirit, to tend to herself and surroundings with attentiveness. But precious little of what will be the tangible world for Anya is up to me. Or her. The lesson my mother taught my daughter in the days they had together was not how to change the world. The lesson my mother taught and the lesson I must keep teaching for her—the lesson I am determined she'll keep teaching through me, the lesson I hope to leave behind as my legacy too someday—is how to be at home in the world.

Orphaned at seventeen, growing up to live what now seem so few healthy years, then for years enduring a body that slowly died from the extremities inward, my mother loved to hold leaves in her hand. She loved the way seagulls walked, the voices of geese passing low, the opportunity to speak kind words to someone for whom kind words may have been rare. What I get from being Anya's father and my mother's son, the specific purpose the two of them together give my life, is a duty to look on every day as an opportunity for love. You can teach only what you know. And it is perhaps through teaching that you come to know something deepest in your soul.

My mom let go. She decided it was time to be done, that she must leave the teaching of Anya to me and to Amy. As she must leave everything else.

"How are we going to tell the kids?" she asked my father.

You stop dialysis, you get a week to live, maybe a few days more.

I arrived home after my younger sister, Ann. Amy and Anya came in on a flight two days behind mine. Through those last days

I wrote what happened in my little pocket journal, finding the moments' beauty and lessons as well as their pain, looking for my way forward. Like the logbook of a sinking ship, something to take when the lifeboat drifts away. Much like I am writing now. For each of our ships is always sinking. All of our loves' lifeboats are always waiting to cast off.

No one gets much objectivity about his loves, but we get stories. Here's one of mine from a year or two before my mother's last week:

I'm sitting in a bread-and-donut shop in Marquette, Michigan, my parents' adopted hometown and the home to which I typically migrate twice a year. I'm writing and watching the traffic. In the booth behind me are three elderly ladies and one woman in her fifties, about my mom's age. They are talking about living fully, appreciating what they have, the sort of everyday wisdom you sometimes overhear in conversations among older folks and less-old folks.

The fifty-something's got a vaguely familiar voice, but I didn't get a look at her face when they came in and passed me earlier. She's talking about a woman she knows who is an example of living fully, of appreciating what one has, who lives with the wisdom upon which they're all agreed.

"Poor thing," I overhear. "She's had both her feet off. She has two or three fingers wrapped up in gauze and she comes through the drive-through a couple times a week with her husband. She gets a cappuccino and they split a Big Cookie and she's always so sweet, so glad to see me. Always asks how I am."

I place the woman speaking as Diane, the day manager at Hardee's. My parents went there for years to grade their students' papers until my mom's troubles, after which they became regulars at the drive-through.

"Always so sweet, so glad to see me." I can hear those words still, coming from the booth behind me then, from somewhere inside me now. "Always asks how I am."

I have carried this story with me like the two green pebbles on my desk. Every so often I tell it to myself for confirmation of what I knew of my mother's sprit, for what it says about the countless quiet ways her spirit spread through the world. When I overheard Diane, I thought about my parents down at Lake Superior a few minutes after chatting with her at the drive-through. They would have parked overlooking the beach and talked easy and slow to each other. My mother would have watched the seagulls turn in the breeze and wished them well.

"Hello there," my mother would have said if one of the seagulls walked up to her door and studied her, first with one eye and then the other. "We'll bring bread next time. I don't think a cookie would be good for your tummy."

One eye at a time, the seagulls on this North Sea coast turn their heads in just the same way to watch Amy, Anya, and me. Beside the beach where we play, the shadow of the roofless ruined cottage is getting long across the grass, which elsewhere shines in the tilting, gold sunlight. "Gloaming," they call that light here, and as far north as we are, it will last long into the night, as twilights do all summer in Scotland.

"Time to get back to the castle, you two," Hermione instructs.

At forty, I finally know my life's goal. It's been there for years, but it's just lately that I've come to realize it is my deepest identity and purpose. My life's goal is to live—as Anya's father, as Amy's husband, as a poet and friend and human—in a way befitting the title Sheila Johnson's Son.

It took about a minute before Amy wept the first time she saw our cottage. Number 41, Shoregate. Built into a hill beside a tiny harbor at the bottom of a steep, narrow lane of cottages. Thick, whitewashed walls and a red tile roof. Seven windows and a glossy-red front door, all facing the harbor and the sea beyond.

We were jet lagged and exhausted when I opened that red door to the homey, musty smell of an old interior on a damp coast. Amy and Anya stepped inside, and I followed them into the low-ceilinged kitchen and the living room with its stone fireplace, up the stairs to the bathroom (where I pointed out, "You can sit in the tub and look out at the sea") and the two bedrooms, ours with another fireplace and nineteenth-century oil paintings in gilded frames.

Understand, we lived the first year of Anya's life in a tiny cabin with no electricity. Even now we are not people with the means to have nineteenth-century oil paintings on the walls of a seventeenth-century cottage with antique furniture and a view of the sea. For the previous six months, we'd lived on my income from teaching college and every cent of Amy's salary as a social worker had gone into the bank to get us here.

When I had come alone in May, scouting for somewhere for us to live, I'd found this place my first day, less than five hours after landing. I'd driven my black rental Saab to Crail, the village circled in red marker out at the end of the Fife peninsula on my huge map, pulled down the narrow lane, and parked beside the harbor. The little white cottage facing the harbor and sea had looked like a postcard (a cliché expression, I know, but in fact, I have since seen the cottage *on a postcard*, as well as a jigsaw puzzle and a calendar). The inside—the fireplaces and French paintings, the old wood furniture, the view of the sea out every window—had looked like the intimate stage setting for some magical, old play. The owner had never let it out before. The rent would be high but far less than she could have gotten letting it out by the week. And we'd saved just enough to cover it.

When Amy, Anya, and I were all finally there together and I'd finished showing off our new home to them, I led Amy over to the window in our bedroom.

"When the haar clears," I said, showing off the Scots vernacular I'd learned for sea fog, "we'll be able to see the Isle of May five miles out. The lighthouse starts at dusk. You can see it from every window in the cottage."

She turned and hugged me. "It's perfect." I heard the catch in her voice, and when she looked up at me she had to wipe her eyes.

My mother was born in southern California and spent her childhood in sight of the Pacific, but her entire adult life was lived far from the ocean. Lake Superior, with its seagulls and waves and occasional ships on the horizon, became her surrogate, inland sea, and she grew to love it. The smell of saltwater, though, the brine in the breeze and on your hands all day—my mother never stopped missing that smell.

"Bring me some shells, just a couple," she would tell Amy whenever the two of us were departing for some seacoast trip. "And don't wash them."

Amy loves to beachcomb and always obliged. She brought my mother back grocery bags filled with that maritime smell on shells and sand dollars and driftwood.

So I have given my family and myself this. The sea. The coast of Fife, a three-hundred-and-seventy-some-year-old cottage, a little village into which we might weave a bit of our lives, and the Isle of May's lighthouse light every evening. It's all outward, all material variables, dreamlike as it is. Certainly my mother would approve. But it's my deepest desire that this place will be just the setting. My deepest desire is that my mother would also approve of what happens among us, of how we love one another and how we live with the year we'll have here.

A day or two ago our landlady, Isabelle, wrote to tell us her neighbors in London would be staying a couple weeks in the cottage next door to us. The father, Jeff, is an actor with a part in an Edinburgh play, to which he'll commute. The rest of his family will be here with him on holiday.

The family, minus Jeff, arrives, and we have a nice chat with Nina, the mom, who suggests a drink one of these nights soon. We meet Sam, nine, and his sister Eddie, three. In just a day Anya and Sam are the best of pals, out with nets and a bucket, catching shrimp and hermit crabs from the rock pools for hours, coming in only with the tide.

It's another day before I meet Jeff, who is familiar to me at once, his tousled hair and the friendliness in his eyes and voice.

"I've seen him in something," I tell Amy.

"No you haven't," she says with a you-and-your-overactive-imagination tone. Amy's usually right about my penchant for the fanciful, but in this case I'm sure. I just can't place him.

Later, I see him out the window putting Eddie in a stroller, and I notice the black embroidery on his black fleece jacket: a subtle, small "HP4 Crew" up near the collar. *Harry Potter and the Goblet of Fire.* Maybe the Actors' Equity in Britain gets its members crew jobs when they aren't otherwise working, I think. But walking up toward the greengrocer on the high street for potatoes and carrots, I've got it—he's Amos Diggory! It's that same winsome smile. He's the father of Harry Potter's doomed schoolmate Cedric!

Back at the cottage I pop in the DVD and yes, it's him in a walking hat and glasses just like those he was wearing today. I skip ahead to the credits: Jeff Rawle.

When I tell Anya who Jeff is, she is quiet a moment as she considers this information.

"OK," she allows but asks if we can get back to our playing. Before I'd left for the greengrocer, we'd been Harry and Ron. "Harry has a broken arm, Daddy," she says. "He's in the hospital wing."

Two evenings later, Amy, Nina, Jeff, and I are in our living room having that drink Nina suggested. The kids are upstairs in Anya's room, where the bedspread is a Harry Potter quilt made by Amy's mother. There is also a little flying car and Hogwarts Express train I bought for Anya in the Highlands when I was cottage hunting.

Downstairs we're having a lot of good laughs. They want to hear the story of what we're doing in Crail. Amy says we're here to slow down and enjoy one another. She's taking the year away from her work with abused and neglected children. I add that I've decommissioned my e-mail, taken a sabbatical from teaching, and disappeared from the literary world.

"Not that the literary world is exactly in hot pursuit of me," I add.

"Brilliant!" they agree.

I confess I've recognized Jeff, explain how Harry Potter is a part of our daily family culture, how we're in character about half the time as Ron, Harry, and Hermione. And I raise my glass and thank Jeff for his part in that.

I can see the satisfaction in his eyes, though he says, "A very small part."

"Oh no, that last scene when you discover Cedric is dead is the first real moment of existential pathos in the series."

"That's right!" Nina agrees. She says she loves that we're so close to Anya that we share her imaginative world enough to play Harry Potter as we go about our days. She tells us about Sam being rendered speechless by a tour of the set that included sitting in Harry's bed.

"He never talked about it, or about his dad in the film."

Amy nods and says, "Anya wants it to be real. She's hoping for her Hogwarts letter when she's eleven."

"That's it. Exactly right," Nina says. "For Sam it's not supposed to be a film his dad's in but a world."

Later Anya will tell me that, upon seeing her Harry Potter things, Sam told her his dad played Amos Diggory.

"And?" I will ask.

"That's all. We played," she'll tell me.

The night goes on and Jeff tells us about the world of British theater, in which I've had a recent interest. I've got this screenplay on the life of John Keats that I'm finishing and have considered writing again as a stage play, though I can't bring myself to tell Jeff that yet. My desire to tell Keats's story is a secret I've kept most of my adult life from everyone but my mom and Amy.

I do tell Jeff I'd like to see the play he's in, though, and he says he'll get me a ticket. Nina and Amy talk about the time both have spent away from jobs to parent full-time. Nina invites us to use their house in London if they are away over Christmas.

"Ah! See there, I've drunk all your beer," Jeff finally declares. "We're all off to Edinburgh first thing or we'd stay late."

So it's goodnight with more laughs and plans for another get-together soon.

To say that Amy and Anya and I are lucky, the three of us alive together, in love every day, with enough money to get by here fine for a while, in this cottage beside the North Sea, where our neighbors for the next few weeks are an actor from Harry Potter and his kind family—to say that we are lucky seems not nearly enough.

In the sun the village of Crail has a vaguely Mediterranean feel. Whitewashed houses with tile roofs line narrow lanes down to the shore. People live outside, eating, drinking, playing cards at metal tables. Flowers pour from window boxes and hanging buckets and over garden walls of stone sun-warm to the touch.

Today, though, Crail doesn't feel Mediterranean at all. Crail feels like nowhere but Scotland. For two days mist has taken turns with rain. The only insistent colors in the harbor are the shades of blue on fishing boats, the red of the life-ring box mounted to the stone seawall, and the bright overcoat of an occasional passing ambler. The seawall itself is a thousand muted tones of earth and green in the lichened rocks, mortared together for centuries. Waves lift white from the gray North Sea to end on gray rocks. The horizon is the change in shade where gray loses its undercurrent of green to become low, damp sky.

I'd call the Isle of May a ghost, but if I did I'd be speaking more about us.

We've been up haunting the high street. We left our umbrellas outside each establishment, first the little post office where we sent off our letters to friends back home. In the Beehive gift shop we bought playing cards for teaching Anya to play poker tonight. In the bakery we learned that the closest thing they have to sourdough bread is soda bread, and we bought four scones of it, one of which I'm now enjoying at my desk, toasted, with marmalade and tea. At First Fruits greengrocer, it was potatoes and carrots and corn on the cob to have with dinner. One more stop at the tiny Co-op grocery store for sparkling water, cream cheese, and smoked salmon, and we'd made our way to where the road bends north toward St. Andrews. There we passed the Gopher Tail, as we call the pub after my misunderstanding of the real name, the Golf Hotel, when I first heard it said in a Scottish accent. We stopped in at the tiny library, open Tuesday, Thursday, and Friday from one to five and also Tuesday evening from six thirty to eight.

If part of the reason we are here is to learn to live slowly, the rain helps. Moving from shelter to shelter, with each outing between involving umbrella and chill and damp, we somehow more fully inhabit the day as it passes with us in it. We've only been here a week and a half, but I'm determined to keep moving like a slow ghost. Now that I've found this much quiet awareness, I'm resolved to keep it.

I remember how my mother would stop my dad as he pushed her up a sidewalk to this or that doctor's office so that she could smell and admire some small flower I might once have called ordinary. I remember how she'd sit in the car, door open, beside the playground and call, "Doin' great, Kiddo!" to Anya who swung hand to hand from one rung to the next. She could find more reason for satisfaction and gratitude and presence while sharing her Hardee's cappuccino and cookie with my dad when they parked and looked out on Lake Superior through the windshield than most people get from a full-blown meal at a town's most expensive restaurant. And when she felt well and energetic enough to actually go into a restaurant herself, she'd study the menu with a delighted concentration on her face and enter into a little discussion with each of us about what we would be having.

Thousands of times I've observed people rush into department stores, head straight for their item, slap down their card, and stride out like they had a plane to catch. I've observed myself do it. My mother, though, limited to mostly shopping from home, would pore through her stacks of catalogs. She'd ask me, "What do you think of this sweater for Amy?" and hand me the picture on one of a dozen pages with the corners folded down.

On the phone she'd visit with the customer-service person, first about patterns and colors and sizes, but soon it'd be where he or she lived, where my mother lived, the weather moving across the country between locales. She once visited with a woman from L. L. Bean for almost two hours. I wish I'd been there to hear it.

Not that she was lonely or that she pushed, even subtly, her conversation on people. True to her Scottish descent, my mother had that combination of impeccable manners and genuine friendliness I'm seeing in so many Scots in their own country. It was simply that she had an abiding interest in other people's lives, a capacity for empathy based on an imagination that could occupy others' concerns, pleasures, and hopes as naturally as most of us occupy our own. In particular, her empathy and good wishes went out to the less celebrated.

For example, though she was of medium build herself, she felt a particular solidarity with heavy people. A lone student walking across campus, sweating and uncomfortable in his clothes, the tiny backpack straps pulling hard and wide at his shoulders, might bring her to say quietly, "I hope he has someone at home who can't wait to hear how his day went."

Forgive me if I seem to eulogize. If I do so, it's not only to remember but to perpetuate such attentiveness and generosity of spirit in myself.

On our way to Scotland, Amy and Anya and I spent a couple weeks in Marquette, and I learned that my mother's Hardee's had closed.

A surprising sadness moved through me. The chance to go through the drive-through and ask for Diane, the day manager and, if she was working, trade some stories about my mother, then order my coffee and take it down to the park and sit and watch the lake and the seagulls was gone forever.

But where do kindness and love of living such as my mother possessed go? Having lost a premature daughter, a grandfather, and my mother, I still don't have anything to say about religious notions of the afterlife. But when I speak to my mother, I often ask to feel that quiet awareness and that kindness of hers. I ask to be capable of bringing more quiet awareness and kindness into reality myself.

Anya's bedtime story request typically involves something about Harry, Ron, and Hermione, of course. Lately, Harry is supposed to get hurt and wind up in the hospital wing, at which point Anya props her leg up on a spare pillow and says, "Ron, is that you? I'm in a lot of pain, Ron." Again and again, she wants to imagine and act out the courage to go on.

After I've given her a final tuck in, I tell her I'm making a Nana nest. I bunch the pillows up around her head, lift her quilt to her chin, and wrap it snugly around her body and legs and feet.

"Just like Nana used to do for me," I tell her.

Last night Anya said, "I miss Nana."

She says this from time to time. It's genuine. But it's also her own way of keeping my mother present. Her eight-year-old's equivalent of my Nana nest.

But last night, instead of just answering "I miss her too," I said, "She used to call you 'My Little Sprite in the Garden.'"

Anya wailed, and sudden tears came as grief erupted from deep within her. "I miss Nana!" she moaned.

The muscles around her mouth and eyes clenched as she wept. This was her loss too, and the void of it hit her all at once; someone who'd loved her exquisitely and who, at her core, she remembered loving was gone. She'd been a few months short of her fourth birthday when my mother died, and it had been more than four years ago. But Anya's grief rose suddenly like a rogue wave over a small boat.

Amy came rushing into the room, bringing her soft voice and commiseration.

"I do too, Baby," she said as she crawled into the bed and put her arms around Anya. "She was wonderful, and she loved you so much."

Earlier in the day, Anya and I had sat out on the old stone seawall, which curves its arm around the tiny harbor. Daisies growing from the mortar tilted in the breeze, but we were warm enough in the sun, which had finally returned to the coast of Fife.

"Daddy," she asked me, "do you think Nana turned into a seagull?"

At some point in the last year or two, I had told her offhandedly about "some people's belief" in reincarnation, about how it'd be nice to think of Nana as one of the birds she enjoyed so much, a Canada goose perhaps. Or a seagull. But my offhandedness hadn't fooled her for a minute.

When I'm alone running and pass a goose floating on a pond or one flies low and honking over me or a seagull walks across some pavement toward me, I speak to my mother. "Hi, Ma," I say and update her on Anya and Amy, on how my writing's going, on how I'm doing as a husband and father, on my day.

I don't care if this is called belief or ritual or even sentimentality. It is what I will always do, what I told my mother I would do that final week we had left to say such things.

"I'll talk to you," I said, leaning over her wheelchair, my voice close to her ear. "I'll go on speaking to you. In the passing birds."

She nodded a morphine-groggy nod and whispered, "Yes."

So the dispassionate, fatherly explanation of reincarnation I'd given Anya at some point in the last year or two hadn't fooled her. She knows me.

Out on the seawall, I'd answered her as completely as I could manage while seagulls wheeled high in the wind over our cottage across the harbor.

"I hope so. I feel like she's here somewhere. A seagull seems right." I'd put my hand on her chest. "But no matter what, I know she's here. She's in you when you think of her. She's in our love for each other. Every moment of it."

Now, as Anya's sudden wave of grief broke over her, I lay down in her bed and wrapped my arm over her and Amy.

"Nana's here in our family, Anya," I said. "I miss her, too. So much I don't know what to do sometimes. But she's still in our family."

The three of us stayed like that, with the seagulls outside in the near dark of the long northern dusk beyond our cottage windows, until Anya was asleep.

Fear spreads across my consciousness like a change of light across the surface of the sea. Like light draining. The darkening air turns cold like the water. Here, back again, is the terrible, familiar fear that Amy or Anya or I have some horrific disease.

Who wants to admit, even to oneself, alone, on paper, to such mental torment, to such wastefulness of life?

Today, the would-be harbinger is a red spot way back in my mouth, on my cheek behind my last tooth, hard to see in the mirror with a flashlight as I pull the side of my mouth open and cock my head for another look. Perhaps the tenth look this afternoon.

I can't tell you how depressed the return of this hypochondriacal anxiety has me. Since we've been in Scotland, there'd been no worry eating away at my focus on the sun or rain on the sea. No nagging thought—*but this time it could be something*—about a freckle or a swollen lymph node or a little ache between me and the words Amy and Anya said about what to have for a picnic lunch or if we should call our friends in the States to say hello. My mind had been free. Until this red spot in my mouth.

My entire adult life my mother's health was tenuous: a heart attack at forty when I was in high school; a few years later, a rare liver disease that was supposed to prove fatal in no more than fifteen years; a few years later, a strangely bleeding stomach that left her so anemic she'd need twice-monthly blood transfusions. Then, a few years later, came the first black patch on the tip of a middle toe.

Leaving academia for gardening and long, leisurely walks every day soothed her heart. A new medicine from Mayo Clinic turned her liver tests completely around. Her fourth or fifth gastroenterologist finally diagnosed and cauterized the raw vessels in her stomach. Even the amputation of her toe worked, for a while, and succeeded in stopping the gangrene, and in a couple months she was back to her leisurely walks. For every threat, there were countermeasures. Oh, those sweet countermeasures.

And there was vigilance. My mother was reasonably cautious—checking her blood sugar when she should, keeping appointments, calling her doctors if something suspicious came up—but she was also busy with the flowers in the first backyard she'd ever owned and the friendship of a new, dear daughter-in-law, and those Hardee's cappuccinos, and the bread crusts she had to remember to bring the seagulls. It was my father and I who asked if she felt OK when she'd sigh too heavily, who checked her temperature six or seven (or ten or twelve) times a day when she got the flu, and who inspected every blister or cut for signs that this was the beginning of another crisis.

Once, a routine angiogram left her with an infection in her femoral artery. The infection resulted in a huge open wound where her thigh joined her abdomen and later—when the femoral artery burst and spilled blood onto the hospital bed and floor and nurses' gloved hands and scrubs—emergency surgery and days in the ICU, then weeks of lying in a hospital bed awaiting every day's torturous cleaning of her open wound. With saltwater.

But even then she eventually came home. A couple months later I was strolling with her and my father and sister on the shore of Lake Superior again. The sun filtered down through leaves. My father swung a stick through tall grass. We talked about catching a movie in the evening.

Always our vigilance and medicine's countermeasures paid off.

Now though, much as I hate to admit it, I'm someone who has lived through years of periodic, potentially deadly crises. Afraid to relax my guard. Trained by rough experience to maintain a vigilance that, again and again, meant life went on.

I ate a lot of crackers last night. Ritz Crackers with cheddar cheese (maybe I was a little homesick). Ritz are sharp. The insides of one's cheeks are tender and given to little abrasions. That's what most people would think, if they'd bothered to look at the little sore spot at all.

Such a waste of a day, this consuming fear. And after I've seen my mother's example again and again of how to value and fully inhabit a day in the face of *real* reasons for fear. I feel apologetic to her for this waste, apologetic to Scotland out the window beyond my desk. To Amy and Anya somewhere down on the beach without me.

This morning, Amy, Anya, and I walked up to the Crail Primary School, an old stone building with high windows and a skirt of tarmac painted for hopscotch and four-square. We were going so Anya could meet the head teacher, Mrs. McMillan, before the start of fall term next week.

This move to Scotland has shaken Anya's usually independent spirit some and brought on a bit of her own anxiety. As we sat down across from Mrs. McMillan in the teachers' lounge to ask about school supplies and school-uniform specifications, Anya crossed her fingers—ring over pinky, pointer over middle—on both hands. We learned Anya's class will be a blended room of primary 4 and primary 5 (the equivalent of third and fourth grades in the US) and her teacher's name is Mrs. Laing.

Anya began playing with the Velcro clasp on her raincoat sleeve and kept her eyes down.

But when the delicately featured, gray-bobbed Mrs. McMillan started to go over the weekly schedule and said with gentle enthusiasm that Anya's class would have Mrs. Taylor on Mondays for fifty minutes of drama, Anya's head and eyes rose, and she couldn't suppress a smile when she said, "Drama? We will?"

She looked at her mom and me. Then back at Mrs. McMillan. Right in the eyes.

"We don't have drama classes at my school in America."

Anya's out on the beach now, building sandcastles with Sam from next door. Amy was just here in the bedroom where I'm writing beside the open window. She brought me a smoothie made with berries from the village greengrocer and said, "I'm so relieved. I'm actually excited for Anya, about school."

"Yeah," I said. "Mrs. McMillan was great."

"And Anya's excited."

"Anya's excited."

I try to remind myself periodically that Anya is eight years old. To her the prospect of one year living abroad must seem like five years to me at forty. For weeks when we'd talk about Scotland she'd ask fretfully, "But it's only maybe, right?" and we'd answer, "Yes, but it's probably." When we heard my sabbatical was approved, she was furious.

I had anticipated a rough go of it when we sat down at the dinner table and I told her I'd gotten the letter and it was official.

What we got was genuine rage, her first and so far only tantrum. She even mocked us through her tears—"Oh nooo! Can't go for two weeks like everybody else. Nooo! Have to go for a year!"

She knows us.

But since we've arrived, I've been deeply proud of her. We weren't done unpacking before she was out on the rock reef looking in the tide pools and picking up hermit crabs. She calls her bedroom in the cottage "my bedroom." A few days ago she drew our cottage and garden on a restaurant napkin, penned in the steps down to the harbor, and looped dozens of circles for the seawall stones on top of which she drew a seagull.

School, though, even a small village school, is another matter. All those kids she'll have no choice about getting to know. Their accents and that of her teacher that she'll have to decipher. The new curriculum. It occurs to me that I—who will be going for walks and writing before this window of mine—am requiring her to make a much greater adjustment than I'll be making myself.

The cottage next door is empty again. Jeff Rawle has been cast in a play at the National Theatre, and he and his family have left for London. So Sam, Anya's one friend in Scotland, is gone. No more tide-pooling together with nets and bright buckets out on the seaweed-strewn rocks. And now she has to start school, to be the new kid.

Amy and I walked her through the village, past rows of attached cottages, the bookshop, the fish-and-chip restaurant, the bakery, the butcher's, and the greengrocer's, on her way to her first day. In her white-and-navy uniform, with the gold Crail Primary crab insignia, she was the picture of confidence.

The day before, we'd visited her classroom and met her teacher, Mrs. Laing, a tall woman with reddish-blond curls surrounding her big glasses and kindly smile. From her calm possession of the room one day before it filled with children, I guessed her to have twenty years of teaching behind her. Doubtless, Mrs. Laing read Amy and me immediately as parents way out of their element, nervous over their only child starting a new school in a new country. But like a pro she spoke mostly to Anya, welcoming her, asking her what she was enjoying about Scotland ("the rock-pooling"), and showing her around the classroom. Everything from books to bins of Legos and markers was waiting on carts ("trollies" Mrs. Laing called them, in her thick Scottish accent) because, as she explained, she wanted the children to choose where things went.

"It'll be their classroom tha' way."

True empathy, I thought. A teacher with the ability to see the world through her students' eyes.

"If you wan', why don' you come five minutes early, Anya. Before we le' in all the others. Tha' way you won' have ta make an entrance. You'll already be here!"

Anya tilted her head and looked off, out of the corners of her eyes, as she often does when she's mulling over her thoughts.

"OK."

"And your parents can stay. As long as you like."

So as we approached the school and the little crowd of parents around the cluster of their children in navy and white waiting for the first bell of the year, I was already grateful to Mrs. Laing for some of the confidence in Anya's stride. But some of that confidence, I knew, was all her own—her deep openness to the world showing through.

She permitted us to kiss her in the narrow alley—the "wynd" as they call such passages here—between the high street and the school. At the school gate, though, she gently told us she wouldn't need us to stay in the classroom. We could come in, but just until the day began.

Mrs. Laing greeted us in her empty classroom with a big smile and, a bit harried though she was, stopped herself and asked Anya how she was doing.

"Great!" Anya said, and sure enough, when the bell rang and the kids came streaming in she sent us on our way with an instructive, "Bye-bye."

"Do you want us to come at lunch?" Amy asked.

"Or," I chimed in, "you're allowed to come home for lunch if you want."

Her classmates were hanging up their coats. They were unzipping their backpacks and flooding in around us.

"No, thank you. Bye-bye," she reiterated, this time with a bit more insistence.

So her mom and I waded through the uniformed children and out the door.

How would it go? Amy and I went back to the cottage, and, while we wondered, we cleaned. "Spit spot," my mom used to say, quoting her beloved Mary Poppins. No matter what else you can't control, you can make a neat, clean house for a child to come home to.

But we couldn't keep ourselves away from the school, despite telling Anya we would. Honestly, we don't always hover so. This may only be Scotland, not some chaotic, developing nation, but it was still a foreign country we were sending our girl out into. Sending her out, in fact, far more than we'd be putting ourselves out into it on a daily basis. We came up with an excuse to see her at the lunch break. Maybe we had been supposed to send something for her morning snack. Maybe for the snack she'd had to eat part of the lunch we'd sent. We should bring her some more cheese and crackers, we told ourselves, and a couple of those cookies, Digestives, that she's discovered here.

When she spotted us in the hall on her way to the cafeteria, she gave us a look of mild reproach, took the little plastic baggies we brought her with a "thanks," and was off before we could even see if she'd found a buddy to sit with.

Where does such self-confidence come from? How do we learn to be open to the world, especially when we are small and new to it? And how do we keep that openness, that sense that we belong in our lives, that we are home with ourselves?

It's a question for my mother, of course. Amy and I must be doing plenty right with Anya; I have no doubt my mother's answer would include that. We tell our daughter that she's loved, that she's capable. We delight in her interests and activities, but we also give her time to discover herself alone and with friends. We're empathic with her. That's what my mother would boil it down to. We can imagine the world through the child's eyes, that ability I was so pleased to recognize right away in Mrs. Laing.

And, my mother would say, we're responsible to Anya.

My mother's parents drank themselves to death, leaving her an orphan at seventeen. That is not to say they didn't tell my mother she was loved and capable. No doubt they delighted in her interests and activities. Sometimes, anyway. I don't know how much empathy they were capable of, though I've no reason to suppose they lacked the capacity to imagine at least a glimpse of the world through my mother's eyes.

But they drank. They drank so much they developed liver failure within months of each other and died in their young forties. They had jobs. He was a glass crafter and set carpenter for Warner Brothers. She drove a delivery truck out of Los Angeles into what were then orange groves and farm fields, deserts, and little towns. They bought a house in Santa Monica and lived there with my mother; her older brother, Ron; her younger sister, Charleen; and the children's grandmother. They bought the kids a dog, Snuffy, a golden cocker spaniel ("with long, floppy ears and biiiiig feet," my mom would recall with a smile). They took the kids on vacations to Catalina and Santa Cruz.

Ultimately, though, my mother's parents surrendered their responsibility for my mother and her brother and sister. Slowly at first, I'd guess. But the kind of drinking it took to destroy their livers so young must have soon been horrific. For one person to spiral into alcoholic liver failure that young would be unusual enough. But for them both to do so, and within months of each other, leaving their three children forever orphaned? There can be no doubt about how lost Ian, whom everyone called "Mac," and Florence were. How lost and ultimately incapable of that greatest of responsibilities, parenthood.

I wasn't there. What I have is my mom telling me about a glass broken on the bridge of her nose; about losing furniture, the house; about moving into a little apartment with her father who tried to dry out after watching his still-young wife die in the hospital and how it was too late. I have my mother, with her huge empathy for me, nonetheless telling me when I was an adolescent that she could never, never come get me from jail drunk. Could never rescue me from the bottle if that's what I chose. I have the memory of the fear creeping up in me, fear at the thought of what she must have survived to bring so profoundly uncharacteristic an injunction against helping me, ever. What a vortex her parents' drinking must have been.

I have a picture of my mother at about Anya's age. A portrait. Her smile is a little girl's genuine smile. Her red hair has been beautifully curled into ringlets. Someone has chosen a dark-green velvet dress to bring out the light emerald of her eyes. Someone has given her a gold cross necklace. Had the vortex by then begun its deep, black turning beneath her?

At some point her parents must have become like children themselves. Almost four decades after they were dead, my mother woke swimming in narcotics and pain from the surgery to amputate her foot. She called her sister and brother to her side and said, "I saw them. I saw Mom and Dad."

So where on earth did my mother's self-confidence come from? How could she possibly have grown into an adult so open to the world, so thoroughly the companion of sunshine and seagulls and little flower shoots rising from the soil and of her own children? How did she learn to be completely at home in her life?

There are answers I suppose I'll never know, but some I do. The Catholic Church, for one, with its orderly little school I imagine must have been a lot like Crail Primary: a concrete and asphalt schoolyard around an old stone building and children in neat, clean uniforms. Everyone belonging.

The same Catholic Church later found her a foster home, even if my mother's place—not as a true part of the family but as a nanny to her foster parents' seven young children—was soon clear to her. And even if she would later drift away from the church to find divinity and grace in poetry and the grass and human beings, she learned that we are made for one another. That there are people in the world like nuns who dedicate their whole lives to achieving empathy and responsibility.

There was also nature's instruction, even in my mother's childhood, primarily in the form of the ocean, its enormity and its intimacy in the rock pools she told me about staring into for glimpses of small plants and creatures. The delicate and precious.

But there's another answer, an eloquent, succinct, and beautiful reason my mother learned her own infinite worth and the essential responsibility of love.

Nana.

When Anya was born, my mother told me "Nana" was what she'd like Anya to call her, if she wanted. And to this day, that is who my mother is to my daughter. Nana. But to my mother, Nana was the adult. Her mother's mother who lived under the same doomed roof as her. She was the one who made sure my mother's school uniform was bright and clean and her drawings got noticed. It was her Nana who tucked her in and read her books. Who gave her universe a center of gravity other than the vortex.

Like my mother's parents, her Nana died before I could know her. But I feel who she must have been. She flows through the memory of my mom when I lie beside Anya at night, inventing stories about Harry, Ron, and Hermione with happy endings so her dreams might be sweet. When I do Anya's laundry, when I spray stain remover on the butt of her play pants, stained from sliding down a mucky rock to get a closer look at a hermit crab or shrimp or anemone in the rock pool below her, I feel my mother's Nana. I feel depthless gratitude for this woman I never knew when I think of my mother's determination that I would feel secure and loved and capable.

Like my mom's entire family, her Nana was of Scottish descent, so I feel her here when I look into the faces of old women in their proper dress and hair, stepping from their orderly cottages—all the homes they have made. But far more, I felt her in the way I held Anya's hand walking her to school. I felt her as I watched the ready, confident stride of Anya's step when she let go and headed off to meet her big day.

Three hours after we saw her at lunch, Anya emerged from school smiling to see us, and as we walked back through the village, she said she had made a friend. "Here's her number," she said and handed Amy a piece of paper with big numbers in red marker.

Amy, Anya, and I have this little ritual we perform before dinner. We hold hands around our table and tell one another what we're grateful for. If you were to look in the window of our cottage you'd think we were saying a predinner grace. And though there isn't anything overtly religious about it, I've no doubt our sense of reverence and gratitude and ritual comes to us, at least in part, from the Catholicism of my mother's childhood (and, as it happens, of Amy's childhood, too).

Amy started. She said she was grateful for her husband and gave me a smile I read as thanks for enduring our first day of Anya in school here with her. "And I'm grateful for my girl."

Anya said, "I'm grateful for school!" with such spontaneity and enthusiasm that I knew she meant it, though I knew, too, that she knew it would please us to hear.

I stole a glimpse at Amy's face and the pride and relief there.

I began as I always do, superstitious as I am in my way, with gratitude for our health. And, I continued, for my family. And finally, for both Nanas and their influence on the people we've become and how we love one another.

Marquette, Day Two

February 3 . . .

I had hoped Mom would wake up and be ready, be able to go to the dialysis clinic after all. But she was extremely weak and groggy, only semiconscious through her transfer from bed to wheelchair. There was, obviously, no way she was going to dialysis. This was disappointing not only because I'd hoped she would rally and go but also because I realized that she was so weak, so tentative and frail, without having missed any scheduled dialysis sessions yet. She was in no shape for surgery, and if she backed off the narcotics over the next few days, the pain would be horrid (her hands are really a mess) and would weaken her further.

A part of my brain screamed, "You idiot! Get her to dialysis NOW and you'll be out in the backyard together come July, you gardening while she gives instructions."

But what does she *want? It's so hard to know. I say, "We can go to dialysis anytime." I tell her she can decide to do what she wants, and she breathes faster and harder and her face looks stressed. But stressed at the implications of what she's decided? Stressed by what she knows must be my worry? Stressed because of indecision?*

Ann says, "She wants to stay with us."

I say, "Of course she does." But, I'm thinking, what options does she have?

Dad has told us her biggest concern was what "the kids" would think. My sister and I. She doesn't want us to agonize over complication after complication for the slim chance that for a short time she can go on. She doesn't want us to lose her.

So it looks like this will happen. She will die at home. My mother. Who has ridden through death-infested waters dozens, maybe hundreds, of nights. She will die surrounded by family in her own bed.

Scotland, Late Summer and Early Fall

The front wall of our cottage, the wall facing the sea and what I'm told will be freezing gales when winter comes, is three feet thick. The windows are set back a foot from the outside, leaving inside another two feet of sill, which forms a seat at each window. Anya has bunched a big deep comforter into the window seat in her room, making it into a little bed. That's become the place she wants to be, with piles of pillows and tucked under her Harry Potter quilt, when I read to her and tell her a Harry, Ron, and Hermione story before "proper bed" each night. She can roll on her side, wipe the fog from one of the panes of glass, and look out at the harbor and the old stone seawall, the rows of white waves coming in, and the May Isle lighthouse light winking out on the dark horizon. The lighthouse is dark for fourteen seconds between twin flashes. Anya has learned to time it just right so she gets an answer when she says, "Goodnight."

Yesterday evening, walking up from the beach, I exchanged greetings with an elderly man who was rinsing a sandy little girl off in the spigot that protrudes from the rock wall beside the harbor. He nodded his tweed-capped head up at our cottage and asked if we were staying there. I told him we were, that we'd moved in for the year. He said it had been his grandparents' house.

"They lived tha' for sixty years."

I was struck silent, but it got better.

"My bother an' sister were both born tha'. My wife an' I stayed the first months o' our marriage in one o' the rooms."

I introduced myself and got his name, John Meldrum.

"Same as my grandfather," he said.

I invited him to come in for a look around.

"No. No." He splashed water on the girl's feet. She must be the great-great-granddaughter of the couple who called the cottage home for sixty years, I realized.

"Did your grandfather fish then?"

"Aye. Kept a boat in the harbor. But tha's old stories," he said. "My wife and I live in the south now and come up wi' my daughter's family on holiday."

According to the date etched above the door, the cottage was built in 1636. Today, I have a tough time thinking of it as ours. As I write in this bedroom, I can feel a kind of elsewhere all around me. It's the same harbor out there, the same stone seawall, same tides the boats follow out and back in. It's the same fireplace beside me. The coos of pigeons down the chimney sound the same as they must have for the elder John Meldrum's wife when she looked out for her husband's boat. These are the walls off which the newborn cries of the younger John Meldrum's brother and sister echoed. And the cries of how many others through the centuries? How many wives looked out this window to be sure their husband's boats were among those heading back in?

The past is not truly present in a place. Even in places like Crail where you can see exactly where someone decided one stone fit well on another four hundred years ago. Like memory, the past has no substance. It's a kind of nothing, in fact. But like memory, the past waits to take today into itself. And to carry today, too, through time, in the elsewhere that is, each new moment, all around us.

The past will carry us off, too, one day. One day, we will also be part of the nothing, the elsewhere in this place's new present moment.

I confess I don't yet know how to make the most of that knowledge. How to use the awareness of our own mortality. How to use the fear, the terror that sometimes robs me of peace for days, that washes through me like icy water even now, that makes my hand tremble perceptibly as I write that my family and I are—like my mother was, like everyone—temporary.

The truth is, I don't even know how to *live* with it, let alone use it.

But this seems like the right place to figure that out.

After riding the bus and walking everywhere for more than a month, we finally have a car. We've enjoyed the walking, but the old double-decker buses here sway absurdly as they careen down narrow village lanes and winding country roads. Riding those buses, even on the bottom deck, we've discovered that Anya has inherited Amy's propensity for motion sickness. Having a car means that every trip from Crail won't require a nausea-endurance test for the two of them.

And for me a car means excursions into the mountains. I'm grateful to be living on the sea. I look up from my desk right now and see gray clouds over the Isle of May and rows of white waves pushing into the reefs, gulls tilting in the wind. But I haven't gotten over my Scottish dream of hikes into remote Highland glens where the mountains rise green around me like living bodies. I still imagine that the Highlands are where my muse must live, in some cottage on a slope, always in the next glen over, a low fire sending wisps of smoke from the chimney out over heath and pines.

Anya's named the car Pigeon. It's a Volvo, good and safe for Amy and me to learn to drive on the left down narrow roads with cars, lorries, farm tractors, and those rocking double-decker buses coming seemingly straight at us. Though it's ten years old, it's been so well kept that, as is typical of cars in the UK, it looks nearly new. Amy's charmed by the little headlight wipers. I like that the rear seat backs fold forward to form part of a flat plane all the way back into the trunk, a perfect bed for me when I slip away for a couple days in the mountains. I can picture the way the forest-green paint will blend right in when I wake inside, parked on the side of some Highland dirt road in the first light of dawn.

Amy packed bags of food, asked me what clothes I was bringing and if I thought I had enough cash. She's always been sympathetic to my need for solitary excursions. For this one she helped me fold down Pigeon's back seat and spread a thick duvet flat, clear to the end of the trunk, for a bed. From the cottage she retrieved down pillows and found a child's sleeping bag that she unzipped and spread as a cover. Anya got in, tried out my car nest, and declared it snug. The two of them waved as I drove away from the harbor.

But I didn't head north into the Highlands. Not this time. This time I drove south late into the night. The next morning I woke early to a soft English rain on the car's roof and the first faint light in the windows. I dug in my pack and found my head lamp and my copy of Wordsworth's *Prelude* and met the day by reading, nearly from memory, what I consider the language's finest literary work in the land that largely inspired it and where it was written.

As long as I can remember knowing what a pilgrimage was, I've known I would make one to Wordsworth's Lake District. I was eight or nine when I first conjured a vision of his Dove Cottage as a little, cheery whitewashed dwelling beside a small lake over which the wind down from long slopes of grass swept patterns. Somewhere between the cottage door and water, a crowd of daffodils swayed in the breeze.

Not a bad image of paradise to give a child, and I thank my mom for it, for reading Wordsworth's poems to me and for daydreaming aloud about that place and about the nearby village of Hawkshead, where he attended school as a boy. In my imagination it was always dusk or early night in Hawkshead. Cliffs rose into timbered mountains all around the rooftops and chimneys. Snow fell often. The sound of children's laughter drifted from inside windows glowing with candlelight.

As I grew and eventually began to read Wordsworth for myself, those earliest visions sharpened with detail. Mountain crags and taverns. The reflections of stars on a lake scrawled with the tracks of a child's ice skates. Countless hours I have spent there in my mind. I've read and reread my way over that imagined landscape, talked my way across it with my mother, and taught my way through it with college students. It was a kind of home, the high, sloping pastures and shapes of mountains in sun that shone between disassembling clouds that first my mother and then I carried through the years. A kind of home and living heaven, as it had been for Wordsworth two centuries ago.

My parents were happy but poor—students themselves—when they were raising my sister and me. Our own home for most of my childhood was a student-family apartment on campus. Even when my mother was handwriting hundreds of pages of her doctoral dissertation on Wordsworth, there was never any question of her actually traveling to the Lake District. And then, not long after my father found a full-time teaching position and a little money started to come in, her health grew fragile. By then, though, I had secretly begun to imagine I might take her there one day. Even after she was wheelchair bound and required kidney dialysis every other day to stay alive, in a corner of my mind I still believed we might go to Dove Cottage together. Such is the enduring spiritual machinery of hope, I suppose. We were alive, and Dove Cottage and the lake beside and mountains around it still existed.

Now, I had come alone.

My religious truths arise from loving attention paid to the world and its inhabitants. And thanks to my mother, who bequeathed his words to me, I found and continue to find those truths articulated best in Wordsworth's poetry. So seeing the land in which he learned those truths would be as close as I would ever come to a conventional pilgrimage.

And I had come for her. That's phrasing we use a lot in regards to the dead and the things we do. It can be trite, but it can also refer to our truest motives. It was a motive that led me to my life's mission, to live as a father, husband, friend, and poet in a way that carries forward in the world the sprit of love by which my mother lived. And it's a motive that was a large part of my reason for taking myself to see what she imagined all her life. Even if her eyes were no more, her child's eyes could see the place that was still just a ghostly dawn-gray barnyard barely visible outside Pigeon's windows.

Shortly after my mother died, I began long-distance running, and it has become an ongoing part of my ongoing mourning. So when I learned of a Lake District marathon, I decided that as part of my pilgrimage, I'd leave my sweat on the ground there.

And I'd leave something else as well.

From my desk in Crail I took one of the two pebbles I'd brought from the Lake Superior cove where we spread my mother's ashes. By bringing these tiny green stones to Scotland, I had made a disturbance in the world—I'd burned some amount of jet fuel to get them over here. And then I'd surprised myself by keeping both on the desk when one was supposed to go on the seashore and the other on the shore of Loch Shiel in the Highlands. Suddenly, though, as I was packing for the Lake District, it occurred to me what to do with one of the pebbles. It should go on the shore of Grasmere Lake near Dove Cottage.

A couple years ago I lost my mother's copy of *The Prelude*, lost all her margin notes, her blue-pen, fading-pencil, and black-pen responses that made the volume a dialogue between her and Wordsworth. It was one of my few prized possessions. I still hold some faint hope it might turn up somewhere, someday—grief's denial. But even in the new copy from which I was reading, the long poem was the same familiar world she'd inhabited in her imagination. Now those breathing hills, that lake through which the stolen rowboat made a track of sparkling light under the moon, those vales where a boy learned the wisdom and spirit of the universe, all were spread around me beyond windows fogged with my own breath.

I was afraid at the thought of what I was about to see. Would seeing this geography take it from my spirit? Or would it always reside there, too? Would its physical presence usurp or nurture the vision?

It had been a long time, years really, since I'd felt so much like a poet myself. Driving down from the farm where I had parked to sleep and through the woods and meadows toward Hawkshead felt like driving through time. The Lake District is a national park. In England that means the old cottages and stone farms and barns remain much as they've been for hundreds of years. The only things to tell me it wasn't a September day in 1779 (Wordsworth's first year at Hawkshead School) were a tractor in a field now and then, the pavement on the road, and the occasional red traffic arrow mounted to a rock fence or the side of a barn.

As I drove over Hawkshead Hill and into more meadows and hedgerows, I had the thought that the two highest walls delineating the territories of my life so far are the moment of Anya's birth and the moment of my mother's death. I only wish the space between them had been wider. It was so sweet and bright. A kind of meadow in which I would have lived forever.

I came down into the valley floor and saw Esthwaite, the lake Wordsworth walked around and skated over and stared into as a boy. Its surface was flat as ice in the still late-summer air. The rain had stopped, and mist was just leaving the highest trees.

I found the school a hundred yards into the village and behind a gate, the stone pillars of which held dignified signs to tell the Wordsworth pilgrim he had arrived. The gate to the small grounds was open, but the sign beside the wood-and-iron door informed me that the school itself, now a museum, was closed Saturdays.

It was OK, perhaps even better, to stand there outside, to step back and run my gaze over the arched windows. Outside I could imagine that rowdy crew of boys inside.

Even so, I cupped my hands to the leaded glass to peer in, as though I might glimpse them.

"I've got a group coming in twenty minutes. But I can let you in until then."

I turned.

A gray-bearded man smiled. Where had he come from?

"Could I? I mean, could you? It would mean more than I can say."

"No problem." He took a key from his pocket and stepped to the door.

The first few moments inside, my attentions were divided as I gazed around and the bearded caretaker recited what must have been the highlights of his usual script.

"The floors were slate in Wordsworth's time. These floorboards are Victorian and so are these desks in the middle of the room." But, he told me, the benches and rows of desk planks around the perimeter of the room were from Wordsworth's day. The benches and planks had been rough-hewn timbers, but they were worn smooth by years of students' use. The wood was carved everywhere with lettering that, though still mostly legible, had also worn smooth.

"Students were permitted to carve their names with the knives they kept to sharpen their quill pens. Here—" He showed me a narrow frame of glass on one of the old desk planks and let me discover for myself what was carved in the wood beneath.

"WORDSWORTH" in block letters.

I rubbed my hands over the wood on either side.

His spot was just inside the door. He was happy in this room with its mathematics and Latin and Greek and big fire in that fireplace. But he also sat as close as he could to the portal to the woods and lakes and mountains.

The caretaker told me to take my time, ducked out, and closed the low door. Surely he'd seen my dizzy expression before, the incapacity to look away from the room and meet his eyes, the need to be alone. I wandered upstairs into the other classroom. Here, too, that boy who had grown into a great soul had read and daydreamed. He had gazed at the treetops and mountains right out those windows.

From Hawkshead, I drove twenty minutes through woods and mountains to Grasmere and was soon inside Dove Cottage, where Wordsworth had settled as an adult. Again I had the great fortune of being alone for a few minutes. I signed the guest book, "Jonathan Johnson for Sheila Marie Johnson (MacLure)," and wrote the address of the only house she ever owned, where she and my father lived the last seven years of her life, and where she had the good fortune to die, "911 W. Fair, Marquette, MI 49866, USA."

An infinitesimal gesture in ink. But her name and final address will be beside the fire that still burns in the cottage by day and the moonlight that still leans in the windows by night until that book is full. Then I suppose it will go on a shelf somewhere in the unseen archives in the new museum building next door to Dove Cottage, under the same roof as the ink of those first drafts of the poet's words by which she lived.

Upstairs, I came into the sitting room. This was the place in which Wordsworth and his sister and literary companion, Dorothy, and later his wife, Mary, wrote down the lines he'd mostly composed in his head while walking or in the garden. There was the couch on which he'd contemplated the daffodils. There was his writing chair. There on the shelf were the boyhood skates with which he'd scrawled his tracks on the ice. There was the mountain ridgeline out the window. The view of the lake had been blocked by more recent buildings, but that was the same ridgeline on which he gazed.

A cuckoo clock above the stairs announced it was noon. That clock was given to Wordsworth long after he'd left Dove Cottage, but as an old man he is said to have wound the hands around to twelve to compel the bird to come out and make its pronouncement. The child, father to the man until the end.

I moved on to the museum next door and found myself overwhelmed by things insisting on their reality: a life mask of John Keats, the other poetic hero to my mother and me; the original of Keats's 1818 portrait; first editions of Keats's first collection and of Wordsworth's and Coleridge's *Lyrical Ballads*; handwritten drafts of poem after poem, even the first written copy of the complete *Prelude* in Dorothy's hand with margin notes by Wordsworth. Here were locks of his hair, his spectacles, his sunglasses. And a surprise: a wooden box he made for Dorothy, the joints tight and true, the lid a perfect fit. I'd never known he'd been a woodworker.

I was drowning in the materiality of it all. When I walked outside at last, I breathed relief in the bright air. I strode straight out of the village on a path past huge trees that would already have been large two centuries ago when Dorothy strolled past on her own inspirational walks. I hiked hard and circled around to the other side of the little valley and hiked back toward Grasmere on the southern slopes onto which Wordsworth gazed from Dove Cottage. On Loughrigg Terrace, or simply "Loughrigg," as Dorothy called it, I stopped and sat on a rock and ate the salmon and cream cheese sandwich, banana, and orange Amy had packed in the little bag marked "Saturday Picnic." In her journal, Dorothy wrote of a lamb here, approaching her unafraid. On my climb up I'd passed several, but they had outgrown the summer and showed only a head-raising curiosity about me when I strode by them.

As I sat on my rock with my picnic the sky rearranged its clouds, then opened itself. Dew on the grass glistened in newly arrived sunshine, then trembled with the breeze that came up from the valley. In that breeze was the call of a goose. I looked down and spotted it flying low over the little river that flows from Grasmere Lake.

"I heard them, Jon. I heard the geese."

We were at the table in the breakfast nook off the kitchen, my mother in her wheelchair, windows around us looking out to February snow. A few feet away, taped to the fridge, was a yellowing copy of Mary Oliver's poem "Wild Geese," which ends with the calls of geese, over and over, "announcing your place in the family of things."

More than once over the years, my mother had told me, gently, almost offhandedly, that she'd like to come back as a wild goose.

To say she was groggy that final week is to vastly understate the distance from which she spoke to us—when she was able to summon the strength to speak to us at all. And it was February in Michigan's Upper Peninsula, with months of snow covering the grass. She must have been confused.

Or was she telling me something else? *Were* they calling her?

Let them have been calling her.

Let her be in every goose to which I speak, speaking to her. Let her have been in the goose flying just above its shadow on the water below me.

I opened *The Prelude* again. As I began to read I found myself in lines I remembered from my seventeenth birthday.

> *My seventeenth year was come*
> *And, whether from this habit, rooted now*
> *So deeply in my mind, or from excess*
> *Of the great social principle of life*
> *Coercing all things into sympathy,*
> *To unorganic natures I transferred*
> *My own enjoyments, or, the power of truth*
> *Coming in revelation, I conversed*
> *With things that really are, I at this time*
> *Saw blessings spread around me like a sea.*

My mother wrote down that passage and enclosed it with my birthday card. I'd forgotten. Until sitting there on Loughrigg Terrace.

My picnic finished, I walked down to Grasmere and stood where the river leaves the lake. I took the green pebble from my pocket. The cove from which it came on Lake Superior would be lit by morning. Sunlight would be flickering at that moment on the surface. Or perhaps gray cloud-light would be absorbed by the water. Like her ashes.

The pebble looked so singular in my hand.

Once again, I couldn't do it. I had kept it with its twin on my desk for the six weeks we'd been in Scotland instead of leaving it on the seashore like I'd planned. And I couldn't cast it away now. Not even here.

Instead, I took a pebble from Grasmere Lake and lifted another from the ripples of the river a few feet away. These I held in my palm with the one from my mother's cove.

This time I admitted to myself I had no idea what I planned to do. I put all three in my pocket and walked back toward Pigeon.

That night, one valley over from Grasmere, I paid six pounds to park in another farm field, this one a couple miles from where my marathon was to start the next day. Mountains rose on both sides in heather. Rock walls scribbled their lines across the slopes, through open pasture, and along clumps of woods. The bleats of lambs were everywhere.

Though I'd sworn off cell phones for the year (just as I'd sworn off voice mail and e-mail), I had one with me. Amy had rightly insisted we get a prepaid one so Anya's school could get ahold of us, and she's been very good about being the one to carry it with her while I stick to my ideals, safe in the knowledge that we're available for our daughter. We all draw our lines, even if some of them veer this way and that like stone walls across a hillside. And I had allowed my line to veer a little more and taken the phone on my trip so I could call Anya at bedtime.

I told her about my day and the lambs all around me. I'd hoped she'd hear them in the background, but strangely they were all quiet now, bedded down among their mothers. She passed me to Amy, whom I thanked for all the good food. She told me the waves in Crail were at that moment crashing over the seawall. She'd been out taking photos earlier in the wind and spray.

"It's amazing here, Bud. The waves are so huge and beautiful."

I was glad to think of the two of them taking such delight in the force and roar of the North Sea up there while the sky had cleared down in these mountains.

The three of us said our I-love-yous and signed off.

Again, I bedded down in what I'd come to think of as "Camp Pigeon," my lower half in the trunk, my upper half propped on pillows, and I read more from *The Prelude*. Arranged neatly on the shelf of the car's back dashboard were my pens, journal, map, and the cell phone along with my three pebbles. In dusk still light enough to read by, I came to this passage about Wordsworth's much-anticipated visit to the Alps:

> *That day we first*
> *Beheld the summit of Mount Blanc and grieved*
> *To have a soulless image on the eye*
> *Which had usurped upon a living thought*
> *That never more could be.*

That was it, I recognized. The risk of coming here. A lifetime of imagining this place had created a "living thought" that I had risked replacing with "a soulless image on the eye." But had that living thought, that vision, been replaced? Wordsworth found "rich amends" on his own pilgrimage that "reconciled us to realities." In one day I'd found much to make amends for the same day's losses of my imagined Grasmere and Hawkshead.

From the outside it had been hard to imagine Dove Cottage—in the midst of a cluster of new library and museum buildings—when Wordsworth lived there and it had looked out over the lake. Somehow, it had been a bit easier to imagine him inside Hawkshead School.

The mountains, though. It wasn't hard at all to imagine the mountains in his time.

And my inner Lake District landscape seemed not to have been usurped. I could recall it, could picture Dove Cottage as I had before, alone in wind and grass sloping down from mountains I'd now seen. The inner Lake District lived on, as it had ultimately for Wordsworth, even though that landscape had been transformed, over and over, by imagination's interplay with perception and memory as he'd grown into an adult poet.

Darkness had fallen as I'd read, and I'd used my head lamp to continue. Then I glanced up and saw a new light had risen over the rim of this valley. I clicked off the head lamp and looked out to see the white blur through the fogged backdoor window. I wiped the fog with my hand. Cold glass. Wet. And in the place I cleared, amid the little streaks, was the moon, full over the rocky rim and illuminating mist in the field.

I sat the head lamp and *The Prelude* on the back dashboard and sank down onto the pillows and pulled up the covers.

The moon kept rising. It rose away from the rimrock and cleared little wisps of cloud.

I told it and myself goodnight.

When I awoke the next morning in the dim new dawn, I noticed my colorful covers, the child's sleeping bag Amy had found for me in our cottage. I remembered my bedtime company, the moon. I thought of how I'd spoken easy to myself, saying goodnight, both comforted and comforter, still the son, but also the parent.

I have heard the tone of my mother's kindness often in my own voice. That's how to live as a motherless child, I thought, as blue daylight filled the chilly air in the car. Yes, I am a vessel in time for my mother's spirit, bringing it forth to her daughter-in-law and grandchild and people she'll never know. But I am also that place in which her love for me continues.

I ran the marathon strong. At one aid station, a tweed-clad elderly gentleman called out, "Well done, lads!" and raised and shook his cane as a pair of us passed. So delighted was I to have an old English gentleman say "Well done, lads!" and mean me that I found enough reserves to truly run, flat out, the next two miles.

The marathon was the toughest paved-road course I'd ever run, almost all uphill and downhill and uphill again. And it was on one of those uphills that imagination and perception were finally, for one moment, a single reality. As I was leaving the treeless headlands of one remote valley, trudging up and dripping sweat on the steepest pavement I'd ever seen—let alone run—in my life, I spent the extra energy to lift my head and turn and glance back down, even while I kept lifting my legs toward the pass just ahead.

And there it was. The perfect Wordsworthian vale I'd imagined all my life, sunrays falling through a fissure in the clouds and lighting the river silver, meadows rising to open slopes rising in perfect parabolas to mountains breaking higher in crags. What I'd made all those years, one with what I saw. Who I was and what I saw, for just an instant, as indistinguishable as the love I'd been given when my mother lived and the air through which I now ran.

Amy, Anya, and I were on a hidden pebble beach in Crail, beneath a garden that terraced down steeply from a stone house. Pebbles rattled in the waves' backwash while Anya hopped back and forth between a pair of boulders the waves reached up to encircle.

As usual we were in a play of her invention. Amy was the BBC cameraperson, I was the sports reporter, and Anya was the athlete attempting to complete a successful rock hop in the new Olympic event by that name. After a few practice hops, she was ready.

"She's really trained up for this," I opined. "But I don't know. This is a record-breaking hop she's attempting today. OK, here we go, a confident climb."

Anya scurried back onto the first boulder and crouched like a frog aiming at the second boulder while suppressing all but the faintest smile.

"OK, Daddy, now say, 'She's gonna go for it!'"

"She's going for it, folks," I said in a hushed voice as Amy panned her imaginary camera from me to Anya. "World-record attempt."

She leaped.

"And she's done it! She's done it, ladies and gentlemen! That's a new world record. Let's see if we can get a word with her. Anya! Anya! Over here . . ."

"Hi ya."

The three of us looked up.

Debbie Stamper was standing at the bottom of her garden and trying not to grin. At her side, however, her ten-year-old son, Callum, showed no risk of grinning. He was the picture of restraint, for which I was grateful. No big deal for Anya if an adult was amused by our little play. Such amusement by one of her schoolmates would have been quite another matter, though. Right then and there, dark- and curly-headed, full- and freckle-cheeked Callum made my list of favorite people in Crail.

And Debbie made the list almost as quickly, with her own freckles and her red hair, smile, long blouse in the sea wind, and her invitation to come up for a glass of wine. We'd met and exchanged pleasantries before. She and her husband, Alan, are the unofficial goodwill ambassadors and chief enthusiasts of Crail Harbour. Together, they run a little café, the Crail Harbour Tearoom, adjacent to their home. And Debbie is an artist whose paintings of this coast hang in cottages all over the village. Now as she poured the wine and tucked her feet up onto the couch under her, she told us she was glad to have us just down the shore and sorry it had taken so long to have us over. She was eager to know if we were happy here.

Delighted, we all agreed.

Alan soon joined us from the tearoom kitchen where he'd been repairing the espresso machine. He's maybe ten years older than Debbie, retired from technical and engineering business, and appeared the casual British gentleman in his shorts and madras-plaid shirtsleeves. His friendliness was couched in pragmatic conversation—how Anya was finding the school, how we liked the car we'd purchased, where we planned to visit in Scotland—but was no less sincere than Debbie's.

It's been good, Amy, Anya, and I settling into our new life together. Just the three of us, snug in a cottage on a windswept sea, with an abundance of time and attention for one another. But since Anya's started school, Amy's been missing our circle of friends back home. Anya, too, has admitted to being a little lonely. Of the three of us, I am by far the most at home in isolation. Solitude is where my poetry resides and where I go to grieve. But even I am ready for a community again.

Though it was our first time in the Stampers' living room, it already felt comfortable. Familiar. And so did they. Like friends already. Anya and Callum went up to his room for some computer games. Alan opened a second bottle of wine as the breeze came in through the door opened to a horizon of sea.

Back in August when Amy and I heard an advertisement on the radio for a production of *Mary Poppins* at the Edinburgh Playhouse, we decided the musical would be the perfect outing when Amy's parents came for a visit in October. But as the date of their visit drew closer, I alternated between pleasantly anticipating and fearing the show.

Yes, fearing *Mary Poppins*. I've known every word of every song by heart since I was a small boy and can right now, with virtually no effort, conjure in my mind my mother's voice singing "Supercalifragilisticexpialidocious." What's more, Mary Poppins's blend of "spit spot" orderliness (taken, with a bit of pride, to satiric extremes) —along with propriety, whimsy, and kindness—was for my mother a kind of playful model for how she saw herself caring for her family. This aspect of my mother's personality and self-concept had its serious origins in her proper Scottish Nana maintaining a sense of safety and care as both parents spun themselves into alcoholic chaos and self-destruction. But my mother also knew how to enjoy who she was and cultivated the Mary Poppins in herself with great pleasure—"In every job that must be done there's an element of fun." My sister and I understood our roles as the children being taught our good manners and compassion and sing-along optimism—"Nowhere is there a more happier crew than them what sings chim chimney, chim, chim charoo."

But how was I going to sit there, hearing these silly songs, watching Mary Poppins teach Michael and Jane good manners and compassion and sing-along optimism without losing it? Would a resentment rise up in me at Amy's folks—healthy, middle-class grandparents-on-the-go taking in a musical in Europe with the three of us—as I sat there, knowing that my mom, whose health was too far gone by the time such middle-class possibilities were within her financial reach, would have counted the same night as among the happiest imaginable, if she had been able to join us? I could see myself weeping like an idiot, there in the audience of kids and parents and grandparents as Mary Poppins drifted down from the sky, umbrella in hand.

And sure enough, last night when we went to the show I did shed a tear or two. My mother had said many times that if she could have been granted any ability it would have been to sing and dance, and there were all these dancers, singing and turning and spinning Mary Poppins from chimney to chimney on the rooftops, their brushes twirling with their lithe bodies in silhouette.

How many innumerable brain cells branching innumerably to brain cells make up a human being? What divine mathematics of those cells stored and sung "Supercalifragilisticexpialidocious" and happily kept on imagining dancing across that stage long after the feet were gone? I sat there with the reality that all those cells—all of them—and their branches full of this music and movement, had crumbled and then turned to ash and to smoke that billowed and curled and became nothing of music or dance or the love of caring for a family. Of caring for me.

But in the second act, when Mary Poppins returned, flying in again under her umbrella, Anya, exhausted at the end of a big day, was curled in her fancy dress into the crook of my arm, watching all this, writing it in her own innumerable brain cells.

Instead of resentment for Amy's folks, I thought of how my mom had been happy to share with them the love of my own little family of three. How she is linked forever with Anya's other grandparents in that one eight-year-old person, who was curled on her velvet seat and leaning against me. I thought of how my mom counts on Amy's parents and on my father to go on as her Little Sprite's grandparents. How she counts on me to teach Anya manners and compassion and sing-along-optimism.

I admit it. I'm a mama's boy. Moved by a schmaltzy musical and how it speaks to me of what I want to be to my sleepy little girl, smiling and watching and cuddled in my arm.

So be it.

Those beautiful, branching cells of my mother's mind that sung and imagined dancing and loved us have dissolved into nothing. I'll have to live the rest of my life knowing that. Knowing that's what life will come to for us as well. But I refuse to let my mother's sense of joy dissolve to nothing as well.

"A spoonful of sugar helps the medicine go down."

We don't have the money to be staying in this old mansion of a Highland hotel with its oak-wainscoted lobby, lilies, wood crackling in the fireplace, candles burning in silver candelabras, and paintings and stag heads on walls to the fifteen-foot ceilings, but when I was cottage hunting in May and came to Loch Shiel and saw the place, the Glenfinnan House Hotel, the only dwelling as far as I could see on the shore, I told myself I'd bring Amy and Anya and (when they visited us, as they promised they would) Amy's parents here. The place is a bit of fairy tale on the loch we've seen time and again as the Black Loch in Harry Potter films and imagined beside Hogwarts in a thousand bedtime stories. We don't have the money, and I mean that literally. But we'll let the good people of Mastercard worry about it, for a while at least, while like many writers I know, I pretend myself and family into a luxury beyond my means.

Amy and Anya are under the covers and duvet up in the antique bed in our room. Amy's folks are asleep down the hall. None of the rooms has a TV, phone, or (unless you ask for one, which there seems no reason to do) a door key. A few minutes ago I walked out in the dark across the lawn to the dark shore and looked back at the hotel, mountains soaring into the stars around it. A minor vision was fulfilled.

Earlier today we walked to the high, curving train viaduct we'd seen in every Harry Potter movie. Anya and I stood next to the bottom of one of the pillars, and she said, "Let's touch it together on three. One, two, three."

I touched the pillar, and she pulled her hand back.

"I can't!"

Ah, the membrane between dream and reality. She knows better than her old dad that it's not always wise to reach through it.

She tried again, but her fingertips stopped less than an inch from the concrete.

"Oh, I can't do it!" she said as she wheeled around to look at me and rested her back against the pillar.

I grinned. "Anya, your back."

"Oh!" She startled forward. She turned around to face the pillar and stared at it intently. With only a little hesitation now, she reached out and touched it with her hand.

Later, on the shore of the loch, I confessed that I couldn't see Hogwarts Castle out on the peninsula where it's supposed to be.

"I can," she said.

"I'm not surprised. I'm just a muggle."

"But I'm magic." It was half question and half statement.

"So you are."

Back at the hotel, she played board games with her mom and grandparents in the library. Meanwhile I ran ten miles of a gated, dirt-track road down the east side of the loch. It was among the best runs of my life. The mountains sloped with orange grasses and brown ferns up to the snow straight above me. Whitecaps rose from the blue loch. Loch Shiel. Sheila. A conversation between rain and sleet and tilting-in sun went on all around me. As I ran past that peninsula onto which someone at a computer screen had superimposed a castle, I admit I looked hard.

Rain splattered my glasses, so I took them off to keep from stumbling on the rough road. But the sleet came up again and stung my eyes and then my closed eyelids. I ran on with my hand shielding my eyes until the sun returned. When I turned to look at the storm passing behind me, I saw I was standing before a perfect rainbow arching from the loch up over the dirt road and back down onto the slope.

The intangible. Nothing.

Yet here just the same.

The friendship between three young wizards. The memory of our beloved dead.

Love itself.

The lobby fire before which I've been sitting in a wing-back chair and writing this has settled down to embers. The third pint I've billed to our room, after an intermission of one pot of tea, is gone. Amy's folks would have paid for our stay here without giving it a second thought, but this is my vision, my gift. The Highlands. A stately old manor house beside my mother's namesake loch. Like something from a story I've made up for all of them, for myself, in this landscape so welcoming to stories.

Halloween, and October ends cold. Amy's folks are gone, back in Michigan. It's just the three of us again.

While Anya was in school Amy and I spent a day searching the secondhand shops in St. Andrews for clothes to go with a fox mask and tail Anya found down in Edinburgh for a costume. Foxes inhabit a significant territory in her psyche. Wolves, cheetahs, and horses hold their own places, too, but it's a fox into which she wants me to turn Harry Potter in our bedtime stories. Always a fox. And she's never wavered on her costume choice for this year. On Amy's parents' last night with us, she wore the mask as we all played poker at the kitchen table.

Kids are Amy's great purpose and talent. For work back home, she defends and protects them. She struggles to help their families be kind and caring and safe. She devotes her imagination to empathizing with them. Not infrequently she cries for them. And their little joys are among her greatest delights. Always, it's the little person's point of view through which she sees. And of course, all of this purpose and talent and empathy for kids she devotes also, and above all, to Anya. So Anya's Halloween costume, a chance for the simple happiness of a kid, may well have meant just as much to Amy.

She and I made a date out of our search, stopping for lunch before hunting through more secondhand stores in St. Andrews's narrow side streets. Finally, Amy found a brown fleece sweat suit, a brown fake-fur jacket, and a fake-fur hat that looked as though it were supposed to be fox. Later, when Anya tried on the sweats and jacket she was pleased with the results. The hat, however, looked like a blow-dried fox's head puffing out around the mask. The sweat suit's hood clearly made a more realistic head.

Trick-or-treating itself, "guising" as it's called here, was a bit like Anya had known it back home. The key difference is that the guisers are required to provide some sort of entertainment—a joke, riddle, song, poem, et cetera—in exchange for the treat. We were joined by Anya's new friend from school Emma, who was dressed as a witch, and Emma's mother. As we headed out into the dark, the little fox and little witch ran ahead of us. I explained to Emma's mum that in the US, trick-or-treating is a much more straightforward transaction: a more or less empty threat, followed by the passing of the candy, followed by a thank-you, and you're on to the next door. Sometimes there's a pause in the process, I said, to identify your costume or receive a compliment, but on the whole the endeavor is one of American mass-scale efficiency.

Rain moved in from the sea. I quickened my pace to try to shelter the girls under my umbrella as we passed the small sheep pasture in the middle of the village. The sheep seemed only slightly disturbed by our passing—even if one of us was a fox—and I saw behind us they went right back to grazing in the rain.

Emma's mum directed us through the four-hundred-year-old cemetery. As we walked between headstones she told us for a good fright we had to turn off our torches (which struck me as a much better word than *flashlights*, especially in this situation).

We called at the gothic stone house of the church vicar, a delightfully jolly bald fellow whom everyone in the village addresses simply as Mike and who teaches the school's religious-education lessons, a regular offering in all state schools in Scotland. Mike had introduced himself to me back in May when I'd come to Crail alone, looking for a place to settle for the year. His eager, kind welcome had contributed to my good feelings about the village. And in the few times I've bumped into him around town since, he's always been anxious to hear how we're getting on and pleased when I tell him we're delighted to be here. He never says a word to us about coming to his church, and according to Anya, his religious-education lessons are about Buddhism and Islam and science as well as Christian principles, all of which he presents with equal enthusiasm.

He answered his door in a tall, purple, silver-starred wizard hat, prompting me to wonder how many small-town ministers in the US would dream of wearing *that*. He invited us inside, and the girls told their jokes.

Emma's was "Wha' da skeletons say when they eat? Bone appétit."

She's a shy girl and told it quietly but with an irrepressible brogue and smile beneath her witch hat.

Anya's was "What did the mama ghost say to the baby ghost? Put on your boos and socks." Owing to some combination of Anya's American accent and the thinness of the pun, the joke took a few moments for Mike to get.

"Ah, oh yes! Boots and socks. Of course. Brilliant, brilliant!" He chuckled hardily and was equally generous with the candy bowl, inviting the girls to take three pieces each.

The rain passed on, and we made our way through the village, stopping at friends of Emma's family and new friends of ours. We walked under amber streetlights from door to door, down narrow streets of wet stone houses and cottages, Anya yipping and Emma cackling. Between the time it took the girls to repeat their jokes and their parents to have a chat with the hosts at each stop, Anya managed just a fraction of the candy take she'd have gotten in the States, but she only seemed to mind a little.

Back at our cottage, she sat on the living room floor, fox mask up on her head, and chose a couple pieces before going up to bed. Amy asked if we could see her in the mask just once more. Anya obliged and pulled it down over her face, rose on all fours, looked our way, and tilted her head as if to say, "What sort of creatures are you?"

Marquette, Day Two Continues

February 3 . . .

I washed soiled bedclothes and towels in the laundry basin in the basement, my hands wrist deep in hot, sudsy water. Disbelieving. But real.

Real like changing her dress. Her pain. Her naked, soft body.

But today was also a day of being alive, of feeding her Cheerios, and of her smile when I asked how she liked them. A smile when I told her about Anya's dance classes and how she's going to be here tomorrow and want to climb up in her lap.

And lots of smiles as my sister's girlfriends showed up to visit. Kathy said, "Hi, Sheila." Kathy is an upper Michigan country girl, with little in the way of born material advantages like money or a lithe body. That, and her good cheer, her kindness and generosity of spirit, and her decades-long loyalty to my sister have won my mother's love. The unsung and uncelebrated. How it is to be them, to live in their skin. Their humanity has been one of my mother's greatest concerns and joys as long as I can remember.

She opened her eyes, smiled, and said, "Hi, Kathy."

A short time later, Debbie, another of Ann's friends, showed up. Debbie's wedding was in the midst of Mom's last strong time, October, and Mom was thrilled to be well enough to go. She has always believed in Deb. A few years ago she spent many hours over a period of months talking with her, helping her decide what she wanted to do since she'd graduated with a teaching certificate only to discover she wasn't passionate about being in the classroom. Mom encouraged Deb in her love of outdoors work—plenty of people make their livings doing what they love, Mom insisted, why not Deb?—and helped her research degrees in forestry and fill out the applications and loan paperwork.

As Deb stepped into the living room she hugged my sister and Kathy, then bent down and hugged my mom and reported that she'd just been out snowshoeing for three hours at work today. "The snow coming down was so beautiful," she said. "And I thought, I'm here because of Sheila."

Mom ate spoonfuls of ice cream as Ann fed them to her, and these wonderful young women talked and laughed. Just as she adores them as individuals, Mom has always loved Ann's circle of friends, loved the energy and humor, the camaraderie and good will of the young women in my sister's life. And she was a part of that, smiling with them through closed eyes, raising her head for a bit, then letting her chin fall to her chest. She growled when offered anything—protein drink, root beer, Sierra Mist—other than ice cream. Her shoulders shook with laughter when Ann said, "You're growling for 'no,' you're smiling for 'yes'?"

Finally, it was time for the night-duty hospice nurse to help us get Mom in bed, and Ann and her friends left for dinner out on the town. I whispered in Mom's ear, "That made her happy. That was nice, Mom. Good job."

Once we had her in bed, but before the uncomfortable change to nightgown—even the slightest movement or brush of her hands pained her—and before the change of dressings on her bedsores, we offered her morphine from a mouth dropper.

"Open your mouth if you can," I said. I stroked her cheek, touched her lips. "Open up, Ma," I said louder. I stroked some more. "Open your mouth, if you can."

She snapped open her mouth into a large O and said, "Ah!" breaking us all into laughter, herself included.

It's the kind of joke she's played before. Some years ago, in the middle of a night in the hospital after my mother's first foot amputation, my father was drawing up a dose of insulin for her in the dark while she lay in a morphine-drenched sleep. He was being careful, as always, holding up the little bottle and syringe to the light spilling in from the door, then swabbing a spot on her shoulder with alcohol on a cotton ball, then setting the bottle of insulin down on the nightstand gently, then turning the needle toward her skin and positioning his hand so he'd be able to plunge the dose in smoothly . . .

"Hurry up!"

My dad and sister and I jumped, and he nearly dropped the needle.

From somewhere unimaginably far away, the corners of my mom's mouth rose in a mischievous little smile.

Scotland, Late Fall to Christmas Eve

People stand on the seawall, their backs to our cottage, and stare into the sea. Much as I love to look from this window at the unpeopled scene—weeds sprouting from between the cold stones, crab and lobster boats tied side by side, waves out past the harbor rising and tipping forward to crumble on the reef—much as I love it as pure seascape, the view is somehow only right when it includes the back of someone atop that seawall and gazing out. A lone soul standing on the precipice, taking in everything to the Isle of May and the sea's horizon beyond, completes the drama.

We are meant to be the world's audience.

I don't think of you much, reader. You are a good, constant, quiet companion. But it's essential that you should be here. I imagine you on that seawall, your thoughts completely your own, your identity unknown to me. I've brought you here because the now sad, now ecstatic, now serene beauty of this world seems complete with you in it. I put you out there in the sea wind and cold sunshine and make myself the one who brought you to it so that I might participate, in this modest way, in the world I see, might make myself the usher who led you in, so this life's mysterious beauty might be completed in you, its audience.

A realization. It came to me at night, in bed, in the dark alone, the autumn wind blowing cold and the sound of the waves' slow pulse through the small panes of glass in the windows.

Earlier, I'd written at my desk while Amy and Anya were in our bed behind me, Amy writing in her journal, Anya drawing in her sketchbook. When I glanced back at them, Anya had put her pen down on her picture of two vases of flowers and closed her eyes. I carried her to her own bed, and sleepily she asked Amy to stay with her a while.

After writing a couple more sentences I climbed into our empty bed alone and pulled up the heavy quilts. The sheets were still warm from Amy and Anya's drowsy bodies. I lay there, listening to the wind and waves, tired of myself. Tired of the way an abrasion in my mouth, a mole I haven't looked at in a while, and far worse, little anomalies in Amy's or—good God—Anya's bodies can toss me suddenly into a full-blown nerve storm.

I don't want to stain my chronicle of our lives here with this. For all the adrenaline that courses through me as I shiver in the wind of worry, it's boring. The same old patters, again and again. What's this sensation? What *could* it be? How would the shelter be blown from our lives and leave us exposed to the terrible world? Terrifying and boring.

Think of the look on the kindly St. Andrews dentist's face when she found me in her examining chair, the second time in two weeks, to ask her to take just one more look to be sure this contour on my tongue and that one on my gum were nothing and you'll have a good idea why this isn't something about which I have any particular inclination to write.

But my realization under those piles of quilts feels important, like something I must hold on to.

It came to me all at once: My particular fear of the body is a fear of fear. Specifically, I dread the thought of us—especially

Anya—having to live with the pervasive fear, the constant mental riptide, that comes when a serious disease descends on a family.

I even had to write that last sentence with a contorted, impersonal ending to get it out. Such is my anxiety and superstition. Red sky by morning, sailors take warning.

I recall standing in a Mayo Clinic hospital room, my father and sister and I beside my mother's bed as the doctor, with five or six interns behind him, explained that my mother had a rare liver disease. Mayo had a study underway. She could get an experimental drug. Or the placebo. But this was serious. Years. A decade or more. Fifteen even. But serious.

My sister stood there, thirteen and quiet. There was sun down in the courtyard out the window. But there and then the storm rose up in me. A cold new current moved through the world.

I don't suppose I fear dying much more than the next person. But disease. The body going about its own destruction, the torment of a family, of children, in one's very cells . . .

For my entire adult life, the storm was either gathering, already over us, clearing, or (I understood all too well) just over the horizon. Such joy my family had. Such life. Beyond anything I'll ever be able to convey. But what fear I learned.

"Please," I said to the dark and the pulse of waves, the breathing of my loves asleep across the hall, as I suddenly and clearly understood the exact nature of my greatest fear. "Please let Anya live without that. Let us all go on living without that."

And so I pray now, knowing full well the sad irony of such a prayer rising into the night from a man who has already wasted so much life looking at the horizon, imagining the clouds beyond.

Winter draws closer. The late-afternoon darkness these days has me obsessed with the birds singing out in the harbour (the British spelling of which I seem to have unconsciously adopted). A little research and a good look through binoculars at one of the birds passing under a lamppost reveals that my companions are redshanks, small varieties of sandpipers that gather in the harbour to feed on whatever low tide reveals in the muck. They twitter and pipe lovely and loud enough for me to hear up at my desk through the single-pane windows as I write and stare out at the three harbour lampposts glistening off the rain-wet rocks of the seawall.

I really ought to keep the heavy curtains closed. The draft from those windows is so cold I often have to wrap my shoulders in a blanket. But I can't shut myself off entirely. On the contrary, last night I was so taken by the birds' song that I opened the window and whistled back at them, knowing I was violating the bird watcher's first rule.

Understand, the harbour has lately become the nearly exclusive domain of the birds and Amy, Anya, and me. The wandering tourists have become scarce, and our neighboring cottages are abandoned by their holiday tenants. Besides the lobstermen's quick, efficient comings and goings, we have been virtually alone down here at the water's edge. I had no reason to suppose it would be otherwise when I leaned out and whistled hello (or "look out," or "this is mine," or whatever it was I was actually saying in Redshank).

But then I saw the woman emerge from the dark and stroll into full view.

"I'm so sorry, ma'am," I called down. "I was calling to the birds. I didn't think anyone was down there."

She replied at a volume and in a tone infinitely more dignified than my shouted apology yet still perfectly audible, "That's all right." She wore a handsome tawny trench coat against the damp chill.

"There's never anyone around these days," I explained.

"Indeed. My uncle was Roger Banks, the painter in Lobster Cottage. We're visiting there for a few nights. He used to swim with the seals. You'd have liked him." Her posh English accent sounded as though it contained a tolerant little smile.

I'd been told of Roger Banks, the painter from Lobster Cottage. Up until he'd died last year he was the life of Crail Harbour, appearing at all hours, often in his bathrobe, on his second-story porch to look out at the day. He is said to have cooked meals of roadkill for dinner guests, and he wrote books of his exploits in Antarctica and Nepal. Stacks of gathered shells and stones and driftwood still adorn his little front yard.

"I am sorry I missed him," I said. We bid each other a pleasant goodnight, and I closed the window.

We all have our ways of getting by, some more obvious than others.

Winters in upper Michigan are almost as dark as and far colder than those on the coast of Fife, and they can last five months. How did my California-girl mother manage it? Exposure to even mild cold was out of the question. Whenever the blood vessels in her extremities contracted in reaction to the cold, they refused to open again for hours. I remember, long before she began to lose toes and then fingers to amputation, the white of her hands when she came inside and removed her gloves and how long it took before speckles of pink eventually returned to fill the flesh back in with color.

So how did she get by?

With flower catalogs for one thing. At the dining room table, she'd flip through pages of seeds and bulbs and occasionally stop, study a picture, and say, "Hmm . . . Maybe some more peonies along the fence. Look at these, Jon."

On my own I'm not much of a gardener, but few joys in my life have equaled being her hands once she could no longer dig in the dirt. She'd sit in her wheelchair on the grass beside me and direct the planting. In the winter I delighted in listening to her spring plans as much as she delighted in using those plans to banish the cold outside.

The world calls us out of ourselves. In all seasons, and all our lives, if we listen. With the songs of lingering birds at night as winter approaches, with the promise of flowers in the spring, the world calls to us to open our windows and doors and call back, to step out in our bathrobes, to venture—even weakened and nearly broken—into gardens with those we love to the very end.

For lunch, Amy and Anya and I sit in the car, parked at the rocky St. Andrews shore between the castle ruins and the stone pier, and eat our sandwiches of sliced banana and peanut butter. Peanut butter is uncommon and expensive here, but Amy's folks brought us a couple jars in their suitcases when they visited. I've spent the morning in the university library doing research for the screenplay I'm writing on Keats. Amy and Anya have been at the St. Andrews aquarium, admiring the seals and fish, especially the poisonous stonefish, which Anya tells me will make your whole leg feel like it's on fire if you step on it and which Amy says she's grateful are in the world—because someone should appreciate such a creature's existence.

Our frugal little meal and enthusiastic sharing of the morning's discoveries remind me of countless family lunches in my boyhood spent on or around various university campuses. It wasn't until I was older and a university student myself that I finally realized how fortunate I'd been to grow up the child of adult students. For all the food stamps, concrete-block apartment walls, and broken-down cars that left us to hand carry groceries and laundry, I got to feel I belonged among the long stacks of an academic library and in tall-windowed, empty classrooms on a Saturday. Some of my favorite memories of childhood meals are of simple picnics on this or that university lawn or just off campus down at the shore, even in the car. When the car ran, that is.

For my own rewarding livelihood as a professor and for my lifelong capacity to pursue my intellectual passions, I owe no small debt to my parents and their values. The children of working people, they made themselves and their own young family at home in academia. Though at the time I gave them occasional grief for the backyard or dog or general suburban existence we didn't have, now I can't imagine a better upbringing.

And as my own, new family sits eating our car picnic and watching the waves, it seems Anya is feeling nostalgic as well.

"Nana used to fix me peanut butter and banana sandwiches," she says cheerily. "And sometimes if it was just the two of us, she'd fix one for Yukey."

When I finally got my long-awaited dog in my fourth year of graduate school, my mom loved him like a long-lost friend. I remember the pork chop she fixed for him, the bowls of Cheerios and milk she poured while beside her his enormous nose sniffed at the kitchen counter. But I never knew about the peanut butter and banana sandwiches.

"I'm so glad you remember that, my girl," I tell Anya.

Yukon, like my mom (the "Pork Chop Lady" to him), is long gone.

But all over the world, students arrive at the start of every school year. Some have children who will play in the campus fountains and climb campus trees and pull books on dolphins or Mars from the library shelves while their parents pore over notes before tomorrow's exams. Campuses and little campus families go on. As do dogs and ladies who love to feed them. As do peanut butter and banana sandwiches.

On the cliff top past the castle ruins, one of the oldest, most storied universities anywhere leans out toward the sea. Down here Anya rolls down her window and tosses her crust to the pigeons and seagulls who have been strolling around beside the car.

My obvious propensity to wax heroic about my life has deep roots. I lived the first thirty-six years as a hero. My struggles and accomplishments were a hero's struggles and accomplishments. But more importantly my daily existence was heroic. The feel of a path passing beneath my bicycle tires and the look of the autumn leaves passing overhead, the kind things I said to a stranger on a bus, the poignant way it felt to look out a steamed-over coffee-shop window into traffic passing through the gray of a cold evening, all of it mattered, was essential even, because these were the daily experiences of my mother's child. I was endlessly interesting. What I heard and saw and did was infinitely meaningful. The same was true for my sister. And then, when I fell in love with Amy, for her too. And then, when she came along, for Anya. She was three weeks old in my mother's arms for the first time when my father asked, "Are you getting tired, Sheila? Maybe we should give you a break," and my mother answered, "I'm just fine" with as much truth as I'd ever heard attached to that statement. We were my mother's heroes.

My mom spent most of her adult life studying the poetic heroism of the common, individual life in English Romantic poetry and American film. She knew how to imagine herself into another's skin, knew there was infinite richness and meaning in each person's so-called ordinary life. And she focused that understanding, the empathic imagination, on us. On me.

One of the most difficult things about losing her has been losing that. My hero status. It's nothing compared with losing her existence in the world or with losing her company, her voice on the phone. But I find I'm not prepared to live without being her hero, not sure what it means to walk out to my first Scottish snow falling over the harbour on a November morning and stare into the waves and their long collision with reef and seawall if she'll never know about it, never play it in the cinema of her mind. Who am I if not her hero?

The person in whose eyes my child gets to be a hero is the answer, of course. If I've learned anything from my mother, it's that. And I think I'm pretty good at helping my child to feel that her struggles and achievements, her disappointments and her daily perceptions, daydreams, and passing thoughts are of infinite value. Still, as much purpose as this gives me, I often feel I'm drifting. A film playing on before an empty house on a Saturday afternoon.

But if my mother taught me how to make my own child feel truly significant, I have that child to thank for another lesson that helps me get through. Long after I die—God willing, many years from now but long before Anya—she'll still be my hero. Every November snow she stands under, every street she walks noticing the faces and the leaves and streetlights and shop windows will be of infinite value to me even though I'll be gone. I know this because, far off as these things are, they are of infinite value to me tonight. And because as I write this in the narrow confines of Taste Coffee Shop on North Street in St. Andrews as the fire burns in the tiny wood stove and steam on the windows turns the passing headlights and walkers into impressionist paintings, I am still living as my mother's hero.

In fewer than five seconds, in a dark cottage in the middle of the night, a dream of twenty-one years ends.

When I was nineteen, I sat on the Spanish Steps in Rome, beneath the window to the room in which John Keats died, and decided I'd write a screenplay about his love affair with Fanny Brawne. It would be the story of how he achieved not just poetic but human greatness despite tremendous sorrow before dying at just twenty-five. And it would be Fanny's story too, the story of how this bright, social, spirited young woman managed to find the fortitude and confidence to become the steadfast love of a sometimes doubting and dismissive, sometimes passionately devoted Keats.

All through my twenties and thirties, their story told itself to me over and over in my imagination. Two years ago I began the actual work. My study floor was piled with biographies, editions of Keats's poems and letters, histories of the era, and screenplays of my favorite movies, which I used for models. I filled three-ring binders with notes. When I began to write, I taped the scenes to the walls all around me.

I finished the first draft during a spring snow to the accompaniment of Mozart's *Requiem*, the music that was playing in her room when my mother died. There is no dedication page on a film script, but I knew who it was for.

I've continued working on it steadily since. I've spent almost every day living with Keats and Fanny in my head, hearing them speak to each other. I've walked beside them as they stroll through Hampstead Heath and suffered again and again as they realize that the tuberculosis that killed his mother and brother and her father would end their plans for marriage.

And I had notions about how the movie might actually get made, notions that seemed not completely farfetched. My new friend Jeff Rawle read it and believed it had a real shot at getting produced. He said he thought perhaps his young Harry Potter castmate, Emma Watson, might be interested in the role of Fanny.

I daydreamed of Anya, Amy, and me at the UK premiere. I daydreamed of how, for the rest of Anya's life, she'd be able to see my vision, two hours of what I'd walked around with in my head for twenty years, any time she wanted.

All of it evaporated, the entire dream, at just after midnight last night.

Though I've more or less sworn off the internet since we've been here, we did get Wi-Fi in the cottage for Amy and Anya. Last night, after they were asleep, I allowed myself to do a little research on the British film industry. Sitting up in bed with the blue light of the screen, I searched for BBC Films, which seemed a perfect fit for *Ode*, as I've titled my screenplay.

And that was it. On the Internet Movie Database screen for "BBC: In Production" was *Bright Star* highlighted in blue. Clickable. "Bright Star," the title of the most famous of Keats's poems for Fanny Brawne.

I felt it in my body first. My hand over my mouth and the shallow huffing breaths. My dream was dead. And no artistic death is as final as the death of a tightly topical screenplay when someone else gets there first.

Amy stirred beside me from the trembles of my silent weeping.

"Buddy? What is it? What's wrong?"

I told her. She held me and stroked my face.

I felt obliterated. Erased.

Then, as she touched my wet cheeks, it came to me. A little epiphany, something to cling to. The *one* place I knew for certain that I mattered and that I always would matter and from which I could never be erased was with her and Anya. The sound of the surf pounding the seawall came through our windows with my mother's voice.

You matter here, Jon. Infinitely. You matter right here.

An amputation. The loss of my Keats-and-Fanny-movie dream has been a sudden, total amputation. The irreversible cutting away of something that was a part of me.

My mother knew more than anyone ever should about enduring amputations. She knew what it was to wake with a piece of you erased and the agonizing way that piece seems to linger in the space it once occupied. A middle toe. Another. A finger. A foot. The end of a finger. More of the finger. Toes on the other foot. The other foot. More ends of more fingers. More whole fingers.

As I've done countless times before, I ask myself how she did it.

Early in the story of her many amputations, after months of trying to save her foot, she was scheduled to have it cut off from the middle of her shin bone. Her brother, Ron, and sister, Charleen, had flown in. Our friend Dr. Kosinski had been around to her hospital room to draw the surgery on a little dry-erase board.

My mother's great grace, one of her finest moments—one of the finest human moments I've witnessed anywhere—came that evening before the surgery as the summer sun leaned into the fifth-floor visiting room at Marquette General Hospital. We'd ordered Italian takeout from the Casa Calabria on Third Street and sat around the table, my aunt, uncle, father, sister, Amy, and me. And my mother had us laughing. The sort of laughing that takes your breath, that consumes you. Like crying. I don't even remember what about at first, but she had us *laughing*. I do remember she was making squeaky dolphin voices. Soon my uncle, a handsome and dignified businessman with a native Californian's easy smile and the quiet manners and accent of his adopted Texas, got up and showed us all his Penguin Dance, a kind of arms-to-his-sides rhythmic waddle.

After we'd applauded, my mother said slyly, "We do the Dolphin Dance."

"The Dolphin Dance?" her sister asked.

"This'll be the last time I do this for a while," my mother said and pushed against the table to stand after months of staying off her foot only to watch the wound in the bottom get bigger anyway. She bent her arms at the elbows and extended her forearms and hands like fins at her sides. She tucked her heels together to make her feet a tail flipper, and she danced. She danced around the table. Around the room. "Hey," she said in her squeaky dolphin voice. "Hey, hey, hey!"

When she sat back down, we were laughing real tears.

Having lost her career (boxfuls of notes and drafts for her two PhD dissertations sit dry and dark on a pallet in the basement of my parents' home right now), having lost her health and her mobility, and now on the precipice of losing her foot, my mother had found meaning. It was the joy of those she loved and a simple, silly dance in the coppery evening sunlight through hospital glass.

As agonizing as the sudden end of my Keats-and-Fanny-movie dream is at the moment, I'll find a sense of artistic relevance again. Or not.

Meanwhile I have my loves. As Keats had Fanny. And my mother had us.

As Amy and I drove through the bare trees and shorn wheat fields of the Fife countryside, she admitted that she'd thought maybe screenwriting might take off for me.

"I was hoping maybe it'd let you write full-time, Bud."

"Me too. If it'd been made, I'd have had a shot at two or three more, at least. It keeps hitting me. I can't believe it's just gone. I don't know how I'll get past this."

"I think it'll take a long time." She took hold of my hand. "But you will."

Back at the cottage, I called Jeff Rawle in London to tell him the news before he found out and thought he had to tell me. Jeff's a kind soul. He was shocked and very sorry. And somehow even more valuable to me, he grasped the cruelty, the extraordinarily bad luck, the just-about-unbelievable luck, of the whole thing. He said when Amy and Anya and I came down to London in two weeks we'd all go ice skating in the park, his family and mine. They'd make sure to have plenty of red wine on hand.

"Meanwhile, keep your pecker up," he said.

I laughed, which—though distant and weak—was real and came as a relief.

December has begun. Somehow, the roses in front of our cottage are still blooming. Snow and deep cold have moved down over all of Scotland. Amy and Anya and I wear hats, gloves, and scarves when we walk to the school every morning. Today, a glaze of ice covered the narrow lane up the hill from the harbour. We had to take small, careful steps. Yet those roses are blooming, pink and red in the cold sunshine.

Sooner or later almost everyone goes through life with the dead. The young and lucky, which included me, get away with loving only the living. It's one of the great, largely unrecognized reasons we envy the young. So many of them can lay their eyes on every face they've ever loved. Sooner or later, though, if they last long enough themselves, their world is remade by death. For the rest of their lives the once young and no longer so lucky travel with their lost ones too. Every day fills with numberless reminders, threads back to the face, the hands, the voice.

Among the UK expressions I like is the word "sort" used as a quick little verb for "to make things right." It can apply to everything from your finances to your emotions. When things are sorted, they are square with the world, your responsibility's been met.

The other day when Amy, Anya, and I arrived at the school gate, Anya saw her classmates in their kilts and concluded that she was supposed to have *worn* hers, not brought it in her pack to change into later. They were all going to take a field trip down the coast to Anstruther, the next village over, for a Scottish-dance gathering of Fife primary schools. Thinking (rightly, it turned out) that she could easily change into her kilt once they got to the hall in Anstruther, we hadn't even packed her tights, so if she did dash into the school and change now she'd be freezing on the trip. That mattered not a whit, of course. Her friends were all in their kilts. When she saw them she turned around to Amy, tears already welling in her eyes.

"I'll run home and get your tights," I said and was off. Behind me I heard the bell ring.

Later, Amy told me that Anya lined up and went in with the other children, still visibly upset. Amy stood at the school gate and waited for me to return and fretted to our new friend and fellow parent, Debbie Stamper.

"Well, go in there and get her sorted," Debbie said.

And Amy did. When I got back, tights in hand, Amy was at the school door and told me she'd gone in and asked Mrs. Laing and of course it was fine for Anya to change later. But Anya still wanted to change right away. She loves her kilt. Six months before we moved to Scotland she began wearing it around the house and even out to play and around town, and today her classmates were in theirs and *she wasn't!*

Tights delivered and one eight-year-old's crisis averted, Amy and I left. On the way home she told me how Debbie had used the term "sorted" for what Anya needed us to do for her. Such an elegant and economical word. My mom would have loved it, the word and the sense of responsibility it conveys. The dead we love are always that close at hand. Anything we touch in a day, anything we hear or say can reveal them. For at least as long as we remember, the world that goes on keeps an unseen place for them.

I can feel my mother in me when I'm taking care. Like her, among the ways I feel most square with the world, most sorted myself, is when I'm getting things sorted for my family, running Anya's tights up to school so she can change into her kilt and feel part of the gang, sitting over her homework at the kitchen table after I've done the dishes and helping her figure out how many of ten slices of pizza make one-fifth, calling my dad on a Sunday to swap news (more snow in upper Michigan, he tells me), tucking Anya in after her story, and climbing into bed next to Amy and telling her I love her and listening to how she's doing so far from her parents and sister and old friends.

Sorted. My mother would have said it often.

The adults funneled into the Crail Community Hall to watch the children dance the old dances at the *ceilidh*. A *ceilidh*, Anya had explained to Amy and me, is pronounced "kay-lee" and is a gathering for Scottish music and often country dancing. This one's an annual event put on by the Crail School. We adults took our seats around the perimeter, and soon the children entered in kilts, smart white shirts, and plaid sashes and filled the middle of the room. Two old gents, one on accordion and the other on keyboard, sent music up the stone pillars and into the high wood rafters of the old hall, and the children started in, Anya right with them. Her long blond hair fanned out and turned with her spins, her cheeks soon flushed red, and her brow set with seriousness of purpose as she and her partner, little Paul with glasses and close-cropped hair, sashayed down the middle of two rows of classmates. Her brow softened and she broke into a wide smile as she and Paul parted and she pivoted back into line. The adults clapped along in time until the last dance, when our children came and took us by the hands and led us from our seats out onto the floor. Some of the parents knew these dances; I could see it from their ease with the moves. Many of them went to Crail Primary themselves and danced at a *ceilidh* right here and led their own parents out to the floor. They knew what to do. But we all let our children guide us through the patterns, let them find the music and lead us.

It's what parents the world over do. Teach our children the patterns we know as our cultures and let them make those patterns their own. I've seen it often in Scotland, partly because so much of the culture is new to me and partly because the country is in the midst of a resurgence of national pride. For nearly a millennium, national pride has never been in short supply in Scotland, but now, as the Scottish population contemplates the nature of its relationship to the United Kingdom, the people are eager to celebrate again the patterns by which they live, the movements of their dances, the geometries of their tartans and tweeds and argyles, the literature of their language.

Every student in the school has chosen a Scottish poem to memorize, many of them in Scots or peppered with Gaelic. Anya picked "The Fox Withoot a Tail" (as told by Robert Stephen). The poem begins,

A fox was once taken in a trap
but he managed to get free
by bitin' off his bushy tail,
there was nothin' else ta dee.

Perfect for my little vegetarian with her fascination for foxes and for bodily injuries, but it was twelve-verses long and with Scots vocabulary in each verse.

When poetry-recitation day came, though, she had it down. Again parents sat in chairs watching their children inherit the patterns many of them inherited in this same school. There was plenty of Hugh MacDiarmid and even more Robert Burns. Public recitation brought out the children's thickest accents, of course, and often I couldn't tell what was written in Scots and what was simply a kid's pronunciation. But then, that was the idea wasn't it? A reminder of the continuity of the language?

Anya's name was called, and I could see her trying to suppress her smile as she strode to the front. She got every word, each "ye" and "fin" and managed a little acting inflection when the fox says, "I canna live this wa / a fox withoot a tail!"

American kids learn a bit of Whitman here and there, maybe, perhaps very occasionally some Dickinson, but I'd seen nothing like this back home, every child in the village school learning a poem by heart, a new poem every year, to be said before an audience at a public-recitation day.

The poet in me was as pleased as the parent to have chosen Scotland for the year.

A couple nights later, Amy, Anya, and I walked up to the high street for the Christmas tree lighting and parade. Children had been encouraged to wear Santa hats, and Anya had on hers. Perhaps a hundred villagers followed six motorcycles sparkling with colored lights the hundred and fifty yards from the East Neuk

Hotel to the Christmas tree across the street from the Co-op store. Why motorcycles, I have no idea, but there was Santa on the back of the lead bike driven by Carl, the town mechanic.

At the tree there was mulled wine and soup and minced pies, all compliments of the village. And we were among friends. Alan and Debbie Stamper and their son Callum had closed their tearoom early and come up. Debbie is as big a lover of Christmas as Amy, and the two of them talked about how they might decorate our table at the upcoming Christmas party. They quickly settled on an international theme, little flags and cutouts and paraphernalia from Christmases around the world.

People began to shout, "Ten! Nine! Eight!" as the tree-lighting countdown started. At "zero!" the lights came on to great applause. Then someone led us in three cheers of "hip, hip, hooray!"

I leaned over and said in Debbie's ear, "I didn't think anyone actually said that anymore."

"You got a problem with tradition?" she gave back.

"Quite the contrary," I said and took a mouthful of warm mulled wine.

In the village church a couple hours later, the little choir of Crail children in their school uniforms strode seriously down the aisle to the riser in front of us. As Anya passed, I saw that familiar smile she can't quite hide when she's in front of a crowd. While the children sang "Oh Christmas Tree" I stole glances at the faces of some of the old people watching. The approval and contentment in their eyes was unmistakable. I've seen it in the eyes of old people watching children sing everywhere I've ever been.

Old people and young people. In one wee village church on the stony, grassy end of a peninsula jutting into the North Sea. Every Christmas since the church's consecration in 1243. The old handing over the world to the young, again and again and again. The world made new every time. Whatever else Christmas means, it means that. Renewal. It's obvious in an old place like Crail, but it's just as true everywhere. Each of us dies to sink away with all our lifetime's cargo of wonders and griefs and memories. But even as we each go down alone, the humanity we are goes on. Grief goes on, yes. But so does wonder. New days make themselves into memories in new people. The thought itself is an old one, older than the oldest village church. But watching Anya sing, hearing her voice, now distinct, now blending with the voices of the other children around her, I felt as though I'd just that moment discovered how humanity goes on.

I turned forty-one on my first day in London. The sounds of motorbikes and cabs and buses making the turn below our hotel room woke me before sunrise. I rose quietly and took a run through Hyde and Green Parks down to Buckingham Palace and saw the sky brightening to gold in the east above Big Ben. When I got back to the room Amy and Anya were up and had my presents and cards spread out on the king-size bed.

At the National Gallery we played the game we invented several years ago for Anya in which we first visit a museum's gift shop, she chooses three or four postcards that we purchase, and then we search for the corresponding paintings as we tour the collection. As she always does, she chose images of animals—a white deer in the Medieval panels *Wilton Diptych*, a detail of the tiger in Rousseau's *Surprised!*, and the horse in George Stubbs's *Whistlejacket*. While Anya searched these out, holding open the gallery map, Amy and I got to take in the passing works. We stopped her now and then to admire something—she especially appreciated Van Gogh's *Sunflowers*—but then she'd be back on the hunt, map in one hand, postcard in the other.

To her delight, the horse in *Whistlejacket* turned out to be both life-size and incredibly lifelike. As she stood beneath its sinewy, vein-marbled legs I wandered across the room to the Turners on the opposite wall—*Rain, Steam and Speed—The Great Western Railway; The Evening Star; Margate, from the Sea*—paintings I'd known from reproductions in my own childhood. Down the wall a bit was John Constable's *The Hay Wain*, with its cottage and dog and farmers driving a wagon through a pond. My parents had checked out a print of *The Hay Wain* from a university library once and hung it for a while on our apartment wall. Now when I stood before the original I recalled the hauntingly familiar details—the red and brown spots on the English setter, the weathered gray wood spokes on the wagon wheels.

My mother never saw these originals, of course. Just as she never saw Grasmere Lake or Dove Cottage. From my parents, I learned to love art and study, and I learned the moves it took to turn my love of art and study into a great job with research-travel budgets and year-long sabbaticals. The children of working people, my parents had to learn those university moves for themselves. My father was nearly my age when he got his first teaching position, and my mother's health unraveled too much for her to finish her PhD. She was fifty-two before they bought their first (and only) house. She never got to see the places that inspired the poems she loved or the originals of the paintings she studied in books and hung in prints on our student-family-apartment walls.

My mother's joy came instead from the spirit of the works, Wordsworth's word-built Grasmere in her mind as she walked across campus, the thought of Turner's clouds when she looked at her own sky. Hers was the dizzy pleasure of the seminar room abuzz with conversation, the after-hours thunking of the keys of a typewriter chained to the desk in a teaching assistant bullpen office as she spoke back to the art that had renewed the world for the orphaned daughter of alcoholics.

Then, when her health began its long slide and she no longer had the energy or endurance for advanced scholarship or teaching, she boxed up her two unfinished dissertation manuscripts and bought flowers. With dozens of planter boxes and pots she turned the little deck of our apartment into a sanctuary of colors and scents and riotous blossoms. My sister recently reminded me of our mom's tulips that still bloom from a narrow strip of earth beside that apartment every spring. A tiny moment of cheer in someone's day from an anonymous gardener not quite gone.

When my mother and father finally bought their little house, she did the same for the backyard. With no bitterness that I ever witnessed, she let all her academic aspirations go and turned the precious health and energy she had left to those flowers. And to my father and sister and me. And to living inside each day as it came. The rest of us got where we wanted to go in our careers, and my mother reveled in our successes, participated in them as she participated in each opening rose and pansy. Each of our triumphs was her triumph. She encouraged, coached, and believed in the things we did. She proofread and gave me feedback on every academic paper I wrote and did the same for my sister. Whenever she was well enough, she'd mark my dad's students' papers for him. "It's something I can do to contribute and I like doing it," she'd say. I remember her sitting in the last years of her life in a chair in the kidney-dialysis unit—a tube out, her blood turning through the machine beside her, a tube in—and a stack of those student papers on her lap, a yellow plastic mechanical pencil in her hand. For every paper, no matter how clunky or downright poor the prose, she found something encouraging to write in the margin—"good!" or "well put!" or "smart!"—at least once or twice.

Masterful as she was at encouragement, it *is* a shame she didn't get a long teaching life. She had a few terms of part-time adjunct teaching at Northern Michigan University in Marquette when we first moved there, and Marquette's the sort of town in which the good one does has a way of coming back to you even years later, a little like bulbs deep in the earth rising again and again to the sun. Nurses at the hospital or in home health saw my mother's name on patient rosters and stopped in to thank her. They told her how, when they had gone back to school as adults and studied freshman composition with her, her belief in them had helped them feel they belonged in college and how she taught them to articulate their ideas and enabled them to do college work and go on to the lives and jobs they had now.

Even when the classroom was far behind her, she still managed to have that kind of influence. She befriended the new dialysis technician who sometimes plugged her into those machines. Diane was good at her job but frazzled by the demands of single motherhood. She was just getting by on what she made. She often looked tired and harried. My mom got her talking about her life and her dreams and soon convinced her to apply for the RN degree program at the university. She even helped her fill out the applications and financial-aid paperwork. And when Diane got into the program and left her job at the dialysis unit to study, my mom and dad hired her to cook a few meals a week and do some housekeeping so she would have enough cash to keep going.

Am I trying to convince myself that it's all right that my mother never got to go to Grasmere or see a Turner painting? Sure. But it's *not* right, it's supremely unfair. Still, for her it was OK.

"I have a good life."

Again and again I hear her inflection on "good." Her contentment.

And today, I remember another birthday. Anya's first. June 8, exactly seven and a half years ago. Amy's family and mine gathered in the log pavilion overlooking Lake Superior at Marquette's Presque Isle Park. When we were done singing "Happy Birthday" and Anya was done squeezing cake in her fingers, my mother—who was already under doctor's orders to stay off her foot—took Anya for a ride on her lap as I pushed her wheelchair. Amy got some old bread my parents had in the car, and I pushed my mother and daughter to the end of the little asphalt path, just before the grass and trees ended at a sandstone ledge over the water. There, the world seemed to come to us. Seagulls sailed over and swirled and called as my mother and Anya threw crumbs to them. After each crumb Anya looked up at her grandmother who threw another or tore some more from a slice and handed it to her to toss. The gulls flew and hovered in the breeze and held the air very close around us. For a few seconds we were among them.

Those few seconds are among the happiest I have ever known. They travel with me, my mother's lesson in contentment, even as my own "good life"—comfortable, academic life that it is—has taken me far from there.

But the word *comfortable* hardly suffices for the life in which I find myself at forty-one. *Privileged* is closer, I suppose. Privileged both in what I have and can do in my life, and privileged in my capacity to value and fully inhabit that life.

My mother tended. She tended the imaginations and self-confidences and spirits of those around her, and because she did I have this life of privilege. As do Amy and Anya, and my father and sister, and to various extents many other people.

Home from the train ride from London, I pulled Pigeon into the little Crail Harbour, quiet and deserted in the night, and parked. While Amy and I hoisted suitcases from the trunk, Anya asked if she could go down to the beach to say goodnight to the

North Sea. It'd been a long haul and we were tired, but what parent could say no to a request like that?

"Just for a minute, then come right up," Amy told her. After all the commotion and abundance of London, it was good to return to the voices of waves and piping of redshanks in the harbour, the only sounds besides the wheels of our suitcases as we walked toward the cottage.

Privileged is certainly a better word for this life of ours than *comfortable*, but *privileged* seems insufficient as well.

Loved.

That's it. Ours are loved lives. My academic skills and career that have given us a year in a cottage on the Scottish coast and allowed us to stand in magnificent places and before great works of art, our appreciation for and kindness toward one another, my passion for poetry, my belief in my capacities as a father and partner and teacher and friend—all of it has roots deep in my mother's love. I can feel that love in our days wherever we go, nurturing and sustaining us. Tending us still.

Marquette, Day Three

February 4 . . .

The day began with artificial tears. My father held the dropper to my mother's eyes and let the drops fall, then wiped the overflow from her cheeks. Among everything her body's failings will take, the ability to make her own tears is already gone. She cannot even weep for herself.

Amy and Anya arrived today. They arrived at the house just as I was wheeling Mom in her wheelchair out to the living room. Mom's eyes were closed, as they often are now.

I leaned down and told her, "Nana, Anya's here."

"Hi, Baby," Mom said and pursed her lips. We lifted Anya, they exchanged kisses, and Anya gave her a big squeeze.

When Amy and Anya had settled in and the house had quieted down, I asked Mom if she would like me to read some poetry, and she nodded faintly.

I read "I Wandered Lonely as a Cloud."

The pair of lines in the freckled skin between her eyebrows showed her deep recognition as they lifted and pushed together.

I asked if she was OK. I asked if I should go on.

She nodded again.

I reread the opening and all through the rest by memory—one of the first poems she ever read to me. Later, when she was tucked in bed listening to Leonard Cohen's song "Everybody Knows"—a brooding favorite of hers—I asked if she wanted me to read the poem again, and she nodded. I paused the song and read.

At the end, after,

> *For oft, when on my couch I lie*
> *In vacant or in pensive mood,*
> *They flash upon that inward eye*
> *Which is the bliss of solitude;*
> *And then my heart with pleasure fills,*
> *And dances with the daffodils*

I whispered in her ear, "I'm there with you."

Scotland, Christmas and a New Year Begins

On Christmas Eve, dusk comes at half past three. The shortest day of the year is behind us, but not by much. Amy turns on our little Christmas tree's lights. She and Anya and I walk over to the seawall to see how they'll look from there, shining in our window. The lobstermen have brought in their traps and stacked them in neat rows here and there around the harbour. For the next few days the boats will stay tied in, and the lobsters will be safe to wander the sea floor.

As we walk along the stone seawall quay, Anya challenges Amy and me to a rock-jumping race.

"You have to jump from big rock to big rock," she explains. "If you step on a crack or a small rock you have to go back."

We take her up on her challenge and race out to the stack of lobster traps at the seawall end, which Anya reaches first. We all look back across the harbour. Amy takes a picture, our white cottage with the tree in the window, little colored lights, the red door.

"I wonder if Santa will be coming from the north or south," I say. "If he comes from the south, he'll see this from over the water."

"But if he comes from the north, he'll see the sign on the chimney," Anya answers confidently.

Earlier in the day I'd written, "Santa, Anya lives here" in red marker on a sheet of paper, climbed on the roof, and tied the sign to the chimney.

"He'll see the sign even if he comes from the south," Amy says. "He'll circle around looking because of your letter."

Anya's letter to Santa, in addition to the usual greetings and asking after the reindeer, informed him of our change of address for the year. Christmas has brought a fresh wave of homesickness for her. Her giddy anticipation has had to compete with little waves of downcast as she misses her old friends, our extended families, and the feet of snowfall in upper Michigan.

Amy's moods and mine have been similarly up and down. And there's been tension between us. When we return from our seawall walk, Anya has a little trouble with the cottage door and shoves on it impatiently. I match her impatience with my own as I tell her to stop and patronizingly instruct her how to open it properly.

Then Amy tells me to stop. "You're turning a fine time into a big negative," she says with considerable bite in her voice.

"Wow! *That's* an overreaction," I shoot back.

And so begins our squabble. Anya sets up London Monopoly in the living room while in the kitchen her mom and I bicker over which of us overreacted more. Words like "unkind" and "absurd" fly back and forth, some of them drifting out to Anya's ears, no doubt, Amy and I both loathing ourselves for that but still not dialing back. By my count this is our fifth fight in less than two weeks. I feel failure seeping in to swirl and join the poison of anger in my blood.

We remain miffed at each other when we sit down on the floor and start marching our little silver tokens—Amy the ship, me the race car—around the board behind Anya's little dog. On the second or third lap, though, somewhere between the Strand and Regent Street, Amy finds her grace and reaches over and pats my leg.

"I'm sorry," she says.

"I'm sorry, too," I return. "I'm still mad at you though." And I am a bit, but I'm also trying to be playful, trying to see if we can't patch this up properly in front of Anya. "If you want back on my good side, you'll have to kiss me."

"OK." Amy crawls over to me and plants a long, wet kiss on my mouth, to which Anya of course exclaims, "Eew!"

I find my own grace and apologize sincerely to Anya for my impatience with her at the door. She graciously accepts my apology. I roll the dice, my third double in a row, and land in jail.

"That's where you go when you're bad," Amy says.

Fair enough.

We finish the day by reading " 'Twas the Night Before Christmas," as we've done on every one of Anya's Christmas Eves. When we tuck her in I tell a bedtime Harry story in which Professor Dumbledore is mistaken for his old friend Santa Claus.

Once Anya is asleep and Amy and I have a little time alone, I apologize again. Amy does the same and sighs.

"I miss them," she says. I know she means her parents. I know she's thinking about our usual Christmas in their log house outside Marquette, the tree we'd have cut from the forest, the soft blue light of morning over snow on the frozen surface of the little lake out the window, Amy's parents, sister, brother-in-law, and the three of us in pajamas and bathrobes as Anya inspects the tags on the presents and delivers each to its recipient.

"I do, too," I say, and I know she understands me to mean also my father and sister and mother, whom we used to join later in the morning for more presents and who, for so many Christmases, came over to Amy's folks' for a big dinner.

"I promise, we'll spend Christmas there from now on, if we can at all."

"If we can, yeah," she agrees.

It's been a lonely holiday, on the whole. Not only have Amy and I had our quarrels, there's also been a general quiet distance between us. For my part I suppose all the Christmas imagery and expectations and through-the-years-we-all-will-be-together-ness has gotten under my motherless skin. As for Amy, she's got her mother and father and knows the infinite value of every year that's the case. But she's on the far side of the planet from them, with a brooding husband and without her circle of old friends, without snow falling through the pines of her upper Michigan home.

She and I will find each other again; we always do. Meanwhile I have to remember to be gentle and kind. To be my mother's son. I came to Scotland with a vision of laughter and hand-holding and daily discovery, the luxury of abundant time with my family. I need to keep that vision bright and near my mind's eye. And be patient.

Amy, Anya, and I headed out the door into a chilly, sunny afternoon. We walked our usual route down the coast path where the waves turned over white and hit the rocks and the sea wind tossed the grass that seems to hold its green all year. With a grocery sack in hand, Anya led Amy down to the little beach near the old cottage ruins to look for treasures. I watched them a moment, then I hit Start on my stopwatch and headed further up the trail on my run.

The coast path is at turns challenging and inviting. Rocks protrude from the grass and then rise to jumbles of lichen-marbled boulders, then the path is grass again, wide and flat a while. Then the path comes to ancient stone fences to cross using friendly stone steps worn smooth by hundreds of years of travelers' shoes. Then it climbs steeply, the grass thinning here and there to mud as the trail inclines where more than once my feet have slid out from under me and I've fallen to smear the side of my knee and hip and hands with mud and even a little blood. But always I've stood and run on, following the winding, undulating, windswept coast.

It's an obvious metaphor, that path and my marriage, I know. But as my heart rate rose to a steady quick pulse and my feet found a slower beat on the mud and rocks and grass and the waves fell to an even slower rhythm beside me, I felt completely at home in myself again. And on my return, when I rounded the last point before the ruined cottage and saw Amy and Anya's two red jackets in the distance downshore, I quickened my pace until I reached them.

And when I did, I found myself in my vision again. The sunlight slanted through air wet with the faint mist of sea spray. Amy and Anya's sack was full of stones and wood sculpted by waves and time. Bright air moved through their hair and across the colors of Anya's stocking cap and Amy's scarf and their faces, the focal points of all the beauty around them. All there for me. And the only thing I'd had to do to get there was keep going.

Two weeks past the winter solstice and still evening begins as soon as morning ends. Even with the sun through patchy clouds the day seems mostly about its own ending. Long shadows. White ranks of waves tinted pink like the tops of clouds. Eager to make what we can of the daylight we have, Amy, Anya, and I take nets and pail and head down to the sea for a little rock-pooling.

"Look for bubbles, Daddy," Anya says, keeping her eyes on the still water.

She nets a shrimp right away. I dip the pail to fill it with water, and she tips her net over and plops in the shrimp, which in its own element again changes back from a stringy, flat piece of seaweed into a swimming creature bristling with delicate appendages. As I trail behind, bucket in one hand and my own dry net in the other,

Anya walks on, holding her net at the ready just above the surface and narrating.

"Down here will be good. The rocks are bigger. It's where Emma and I caught a momma and baby crab."

"I remember."

"But you weren't there."

"I heard about it, though. You let them go."

"And the momma tucked the baby up under her."

At the far end of the pool, as the waves thirty yards out on the rocks loudly send up gold mist behind her, Anya finds two mussels.

"We can eat these if you want," I tell her.

"Really?"

"Sure."

"Mamma!" I call to Amy on the far side of the pool where she crouches taking photos of us. "She found two mussels. Let's have them for dinner tonight."

"Sure!"

"You can eat them?"

"I can't wait," I say truthfully. We'll have to buy a few more to go with them at the seafood shop in St. Andrews when we go in for Anya's Highland-dancing class, but we'll scratch an *A* into the shells of the two she caught and we'll steam them all and have them on the dish of garlic and vegetables over pasta Amy was planning for tonight.

"Your first catch for us to eat," I congratulate her.

We look for more, but soon Anya says her right big toe is cold. She stands in her coat, gloves, and stocking cap, net in hand, and stares down at her Wellington boots. For a moment she looks like a much younger version of herself, and I feel a rush of love for her fill me.

She's her own, separate soul, and I am transfixed by the reality of her. We're alive together, sharing this day.

The cold in her big right toe soon spreads to the others. It hurts her to walk so I carry her on my back while Amy carries the pail and nets as the three of us head for home.

As Anya and I sat on the floor assembling her new ladybug kite, I kept my doubts to myself. In the morning, when the breeze had been merely stiff, I'd talked up the day as great for kite flying. But now I could hear the wind whipping over the chimney and pushing against the windows. And despite our added reinforcements of strong tape where the hollow plastic shafts met thin plastic sheeting, this seemed an especially flimsy kite, something much better suited to bobbing cheerily about in a light breeze. Amy was clearly thinking along the same lines when she came into the living room and we showed her the ladybug wings spread wide and ready to fly. She said it looked great but cautioned, "We'll give it a try, but sometimes kites don't last very long, love. And that'll be OK."

"She might not make it?"

"She might not. Kites are sometimes kind of fragile."

Anya looked down at the kite and furrowed her brow.

"We'll take the tape and scissors with us," I suggested. "In case we need to make repairs. But Momma's right," I finally confessed. "It's a strong wind out there."

Out the window the tops of the waves were blowing to mist in the afternoon sunshine.

"But let's give it a try," Amy said brightly. "Kites were meant to fly, not stay safe inside."

"OK," Anya said, her enthusiasm enough to override her anxiety over the fate of the kite to which she was already referring with the female pronoun.

The winds out on Cambo Sands beach were even stronger than they'd been at the harbour in Crail. They came over the hedgerows and picked up speed across the fields and then poured over the grassy dunes and across the sand and out over the North Sea, hell-bent for Norway.

At less than three feet across, the kite hardly required both Anya and me to carry it down to the shore from the car, and in fact, it would have gotten far less of a violent tossing about if I'd carried it myself against my chest. But this was our project, so we carried it together, Anya on the end of one wing, me on the other, as if the kite were the size of a hang glider.

Already we had to make a repair; one shaft had torn a bit loose from the plastic skin. With her gloved hands, Anya needed three tries to cut loose a strip of tape that didn't flip around and fold in on itself in the wind, but we made the repair and then added a few more strips for reinforcement. Still, I wasn't giving the kite five minutes in the air. It'd be a success even to see it up at the end of the string just once before it was shredded.

Anya, however, seemed to have completely forgotten her concern. She was giddy as she unraveled the string and backed away from me while I held the kite and instructed her to run down the beach when I said go, keeping the string taut.

"OK, Daddy," she said brightly, adding to my welling guilt that surely I'd set her up for a bit of heartbreak.

Amy lifted her camera to her eye, ready to catch what would hopefully be a few moments of joy and, I supposed, thinking to herself what we should do after to salvage the afternoon. Some London Monopoly back at the cottage maybe.

"OK, go!" I said and trotted along behind Anya as she ran the string taught. I let go, and the kite rose straight into the air. Anya kept running, pumping her legs down the beach while looking up at the kite.

"Go Shmoy!" we cheered. "Well done!"

The kite bent her ladybug wings back in the wind and flapped loudly, but she held her place in the air twenty feet above Anya, who—when we called that she could stop running—turned and stood staring serenely up and giving gentle tugs on the string.

A moment later the kite swooped low over the beach, then swooped again, then went inverted and banged into the beach where it stayed pinned upside down in the wind.

But before I could get there to help, Anya'd given a few more tugs and it'd righted itself and buoyantly lifted right back up over her. Somehow, it seemed to be holding together.

And it kept holding together through more upside-down crashes onto the sand and our running launches, though Anya needed fewer and fewer of these as time went by and she got better at giving the string just the right tug at the right moment. Soon she was adept enough to just stand or stroll while the kite held its position at the end of its leash. Finally, she looked down, drew a circle in the sand with her foot, and then sat down.

Cross-legged in the center of her circle, in her coat and stocking cap, holding the coil of string in one gloved hand out to her side, the kite obediently keeping to the air above her and the waves tumbling over beyond, she was the very picture of serenity and self-possession.

"There is a Buddha in you and a Buddha in me," I recalled my teacher saying when I'd taken some Zen meditation instruction a few years ago. "The Buddha is in all of us."

Before long she was running again and then spinning fancy turns below the hardly rippling kite. Dancing with it. Then she traced another circle with her foot and sat down again in the center while the kite waited in the constant wind. Then Anya reclined flat on the sand, put her free hand behind her head, and stared up at the kite and the clouds above scooting quickly out to sea.

If your own childhood was a happy one, if your parents were kind and attentive and loving and there were afternoons of pure joy, it's hard not to think of your childhood as *the* childhood. The *real* childhood. The *real* afternoons of pure joy with the *real* parents. The challenge, if your own childhood left you with a paradise of memories to which you return as often as you can but now you've somehow become the parent, is to realize that this, today, is *the* childhood, the very definition of childhood forever for this new little being. It's bewildering, and at times the realization arrives with a nearly overwhelming sense of responsibility. At other times, though, the realization that now, *this day*, can be the paradise to which your child returns for a lifetime, and that you are the parent in that paradise, comes with the greatest sense of privilege imaginable.

We got maybe an hour with the ladybug kite before her plastic keel began to tear loose and she fell to the sand.

"No problem," I said truthfully. "We'll get her taped up at home. This is fixable. But we should get her and us in out of this weather."

Rain had come suddenly overland to splatter in the sand and fall on the waves and move with the wind farther out over the sea.

"It's fixable?" Anya studied the tear.

"No problem."

"Anya, that was brilliant!" Amy said. "You're so good at that. I can't believe we haven't done this since you were little." It had been years—since she was just four or maybe five. Far too long.

"It was kind of like my first time. Before, you guys got the kite up and I just held the string," she conjured from some combination of recollection and imagination.

"We'll do this more now," Amy said.

"Can we?"

"Absolutely," Amy pledged. "This is one of the things I daydreamed about when I was pregnant with you."

It's a fine thing to suddenly be filled with desire for your wife, wind in her hair, rain pelting her puffy coat and soaking into her blue jeans. Sometimes it comes along so suddenly and forcefully I can hardly believe I'm standing there looking at her.

"What else did you daydream about?" Anya asked Amy as we walked back down the beach toward the car.

"Lots of things, and it keeps changing as you get older."

"But when you were *pregnant*?" Anya pressed, clearly intrigued by this notion of daydreams in which she'd starred, still unnamed and in utero, her gender unknown to us.

"Washing you in the sink, with help from your Nana," I offered.

"I remember you said that."

"I did," Amy said. "And reading to you and singing with you. And flying a kite with you, just like today."

"Your dream came true?" Anya said, as much statement as question.

"It did."

Back in Pigeon we warmed up with the heater on while I changed into my running coat. Amy asked if I was sure I wanted to run home as rain smacked the roof and windows.

"I'll be fine, I like to run in weather."

"But, Daddy," Anya chimed in from the back seat, "everything it does outside is weather."

"That's true."

"So you like to run in everything."

"Well, not lightning. I try not to run in lightning."

"So you don't like to run in weather, just *some* weather."

Amy leaned over and spoke softly, "We're in the literal phase, I'd say."

"Hmm," I concurred.

"Right, Sweetie," I answered Anya. "Very good. Weather like rain and wind. Those I like." Though looking out I had to admit, if only to myself, a nice dry drive back to the cottage had its appeal.

But out I went and away they drove with smiles and waves.

Five miles of coast later and one more to go, the sky cleared again. The backsides of the rainclouds that had moved offshore shone pink over the sea as the sun set from around the bend at Fife Ness, the most easterly point on this stretch of coast.

Another thing about a happy childhood. It can teach you to continue building a paradise of memories for yourself, to notice and live inside the passing moments. Though the purely unself-conscious experiences open only to a child are behind you, you can get close. You are the same person who once knew the world so directly through your eyes and hands and feet, who felt so perfectly at home, and you can feel something like that again.

Through the waves' constant churn and wash, a flock of grazing Shetland sheep heard me splashing along the muddy path and parted to let me run through. Redshanks piped out their songs and skimmed along the wave tops. I passed a flat patch of grass atop some rocks where Amy and I had picnicked in August while Anya'd spent one of her first days in her new school.

Back at the cottage, after I'd taken a hot bath and while Amy and I were fixing dinner, she told me she'd teared up for a few minutes, watching Anya fly the ladybug kite on Cambo Sands.

"It really was just like I'd pictured it when I was pregnant. Even before, when I used to think about having a kid." She stood at the stove while I chopped vegetables beside her.

And still later, when Anya's teeth were brushed and she was in her pajamas and we were playing one more game of Sleeping Queens before bed, Amy mentioned how much she'd loved our kite-flying adventure.

Anya paused before turning over the next card from the stack. She cocked her head and looked contemplatively away out of the corner of her eye.

I could see her mulling over the new memory. The experience had already become another place she could always go in her mind. The ladybug kite swaying in the wind, the surprise and delight in her parents' voices, the circle she'd drawn in the sand and sat inside had already taken their places in *the* childhood as she'll always know it.

"I wish we were still doing that," she said.

Marquette, Day Three Continues

February 4, continued . . .

Mom was in bed for the night, and Aunt Charleen was lying beside her. Mom woke and opened her eyes. Charleen said, "I love you," and Mom answered her little sister, "I love you, too, Charleen."

Then she said her hands hurt. We brought more morphine. Sweet morphine.

When Mom was asleep again, my own little sister, Ann, and I sat on the sofa looking at old pictures from our childhood and from before our childhood. Here were our cool mom and dad in a garage apartment in Irvine. Dad was reading Ulysses. *For his graduation Mom gave him the book, along with* Doctor Zhivago. *Outside the door of the apartment, there were lawn chairs and an ashtray.*

I'd never noticed before how truly beautiful Mom was in these pictures.

Earlier, when we were getting her into bed, preparing to transfer her so delicately, so carefully from her wheelchair, using a contraption that looks like an engine hoist, I'd thought I'd done everything right, slowly, gingerly getting her strapped in the harness, but I'd forgotten about her wheelchair seat belt.

Like the transfer hoist, the seat belt is a recent necessity; even sliced and sliced again from her extremities inward, she's managed to stay relatively mobile with just the help of my dad. But when she declined the amputation of her hands and called an end to the dialysis, hospice came to the house with the things she would need now: the little bottle of morphine with the eye-dropper-like squeeze tube for under her tongue, the lift, a hospital bed for the living room. She's declined the use of the hospital bed, thank God, and kept that last realm of independent life, her own bed.

But as we were cranking the hoist to lift her from her wheelchair and put her there, she gave a small moan. Most movement hurts her at least a little, but Mom has a tolerance for pain unlike anything I've seen. This was something even more than the usual ache.

The seat belt! It had been hidden under a pillow on her lap.

I lowered the hoist, and Dad unbuckled her.

When that was over and we had her up and swinging slowly, suspended from chair to bed, she opened her eyes and looked at me.

"How are you doing, Ma?"

Her pupils were tiny in their seas of green iris.

"How are you doing with all this?"

She looked at me with "please hear me out there" on her face and said, "Weird."

Scotland, Midwinter

Amy and I got Anya to school and drove up to St. Andrews where Amy has volunteered to facilitate a parenting group. I kissed her good-bye and double-checked that she had bus fare to get back to the cottage. When she got out, I caught a look at her, beautiful and smiling in the sun. She's on the petite side, a bit girlish looking even, with brown bangs (or "fringe" in the better word they use here), dimples when she smiles, and a soft spot for me that compelled her to kiss me again through the driver's window.

"Have a good time in the mountains, Bud," she said.

Amy's also among the toughest and steadiest people I know, a social worker who—back in the States—carries dog treats to toss to the pit bulls when she steps through the door to check on some of her clients' kids in the roughest neighborhoods in town. Even over here she was on her way to spend the coming day at her volunteer job leading a counseling group for stressed-out parents.

I married exactly the right person, I thought to myself, as she stood, shielding her green eyes from the sun, waving her other hand as I drove away.

I was off to the Highlands again. Among the birthday presents Amy and Anya had given me in December was a couple nights at an inn where I could walk in the hills.

"No sleeping in the car," Amy had said.

"We want you to get a comfy hotel, Daddy!" Anya had chimed in.

The thought that I'd married exactly the right person stayed and traveled with me as I headed north and west toward Glen Coe, arguably the most dramatic mountain valley in all of Scotland. Already, I couldn't recall a birthday present I'd liked more.

To my way of seeing, the Scottish Highlands are the most sensual place on Earth. The land slopes and curves like a body down through vast open heather and bracken interrupted here and there by dark woods. There seems no distinction between flora and geology, everything—rock and moss and grass alike—exudes fertility as the mists and rains move through and close and open again to the tilting sun.

The next morning, I drove from the inn to the base of the mountain on the opposite side of the glen, Meall Mór. The weather was predicted to turn, but for the moment at least, it was fair. If I could find a gentle way up, and if the weather held, the climb could be magnificent.

In spite of my intentions simply to hike to the summit, though, things got increasingly technical—and steep. Wet grass and dead bracken gave way to snow-marbled rock and grass, then just snow and rock. Without having meant to, I was soon climbing, hoisting myself over the rock outcroppings, kicking little footholds into the snow. A quick map check showed I'd gotten a little east of the route I'd planned. A classic mistake. I'd even felt it happening, my drift to the left, but the going had seemed better that way. Until it hadn't. Then there was just a steep bit to get over to a gentler incline. And then another steep bit, a bit larger. And then there were no gentler inclines.

The foolhardiness of what I was doing came to me all at once. If I took a tumble I might not be able to stop my downward slide. I sensed how high I'd let myself get on this steep slope. As I puzzled over the obstacle I felt a chill in the wind. And hadn't the light been a bit less bright the last few minutes? Had the clouds that were moving so fast over the slope above and into the glen gotten a little gray? I recalled that the Highlands kill an average of twenty people a year, often with weather and often on days that start out looking fair. It was time to face a glance back down.

Yep, the wrong stumble and I'd be in real trouble. The mountain fell away beneath me, a steep snowfield with a few rocks jutting out just to make things worse. I had put off dealing with the reality of my situation in the hope that I would top out onto a shallower pitch and could look down and say, "Wow, that was dicey" before pressing on.

But I hadn't topped out. And I had to admit I wasn't sure how much farther up I had to go until I would.

I should have known better. Back at the inn, I'd told the little old lady at the desk where I was going and that I'd return by dark. She'd kindly filled out a yellow rescue-information sheet for me. She asked me what gear I had and checked off the boxes beside "Winter Clothes" and "Food and Water" and "Map and Compass" and "Cell Phone" but not for "Torch" or "Whistle" or "Sleeping Bag," which I was confident I wouldn't need anyway.

Now I wasn't so sure. I dug in my pocket for Amy's cell phone. Though I'd been ambivalent about taking it, I was tremendously glad to have it now. At least if I fell and remained conscious it wouldn't be dark before someone would come looking for me.

That is, if I got reception. I powered up the phone. Nope. No bars.

It was then I heard the hiss coming from above me.

In addition to my concerns about the weather and risk of a fall, I'd been thinking about avalanches. Not having scoped the mountain face from a distance, I had no idea what kind of snow loads might be hanging precariously up there.

Truly foolhardy. I imagined how those reading of my demise in the paper might shake their heads and say, "He should have known better."

The hiss got louder. I had just enough time to wonder if avalanches make this sound as I squinted up the slope.

Sleet.

And as quick as an avalanche, the sleet was over me. I flipped up my hood, and the icy swarm pelted down. In seconds the glen far below and the mountains opposite were gone in a wash of white. The wind gusted hard, and just as quickly as the sleet had come it turned to snow.

The glorious fact that the hiss hadn't been an avalanche didn't mean the risk was over, though. Now there would be a fresh layer of snow on ice-crusted snow, an avalanche-prone combination if the new accumulation built up. Not only was this foolhardy, I admitted to myself, it was selfish. Was this how I took care of the dad Anya loves and needs? The partner Amy counts on to raise her with? Is this what my mom would have wanted for her son when she taught him to look for the sublime?

So, it would be back down. No matter how close above a gentle angle might be or how much safer a north-side descent looked on the map, I couldn't risk going any higher.

"I'll see you in June," I told the mountain and took off my pack to retrieve my spare pair of dry gloves, my down coat, and second hat. I would follow my footsteps back down. That would at least keep me on a route of footholds that had held on the way up. If I could get off the steep snowfields and rock, down to the grass and bracken, I'd be OK, even in a complete blizzard. Blizzards I can do. You just follow the descent, keep your head down, and keep moving. Sooner or later I would come to the road through the glen. *If* I could get off the steep, high slope.

And then—in the time it took me to pull out and put on my dry gloves, down jacket, and extra hat; hoist my pack to my back; and down-climb not ten feet—the sky cleared. And then the clouds were moving out of the glen below, racing out of it, up the sides of the opposite mountains. I recognized the stand of woods, tiny and distant, above the inn. And then the sun broke for a moment and lit the snow-covered peaks and the green woods and the silver river Coe and the lower slopes that rise yellow, green, and brown with the smooth, sensuous curves of a body.

"OK," I said aloud. "What now?" I looked up the slope. I looked back down.

I wished I had an altimeter. Without one, I just couldn't tell how far up the map's closely bunched contour lines I'd already come and how many of them I had left.

But I *did* know that back the way I'd come was a long, precarious climb down. If the break in the weather held, I might safely reach a gentler escape route to the north in just a few more minutes of ascending. I turned around and climbed again. After some deliberation, I found routes up each rock outcropping and, with my breath held, managed to get over them without pitching backward.

There was more steep going ahead. Soon I was sinking in snow past my knees. Thoughts of avalanche returned, joined by a new fear of deep fissures in the mountain hidden under the snow. My God, I thought, I'd been an idiot to let myself get into this.

And then the slope wasn't so sheer. And then I was moving without my hands, as if going up stairs instead of a ladder.

The clouds darkened again. This time they brought wind with thin snow flurries. But like blizzards, wind I could do—step after tilting step into it. And stay well back from anything off which you wouldn't want to get blown.

It was a long walk up one false summit and then another, and, though it was just walking now, all the while the wind and my exposure to it was getting worse. Up there, what little snow clung to the rocks looked plastered on with serrated trowels. The gusts rocked me back, and I almost lost my balance several times. I had to bow my head all the way over to keep the snow from blasting my eyes like sand.

The summit ridge took me a couple hundred yards beyond my escape route, but I'd come this far. On the other hand, a not uncommon end climbers meet on some relatively straightforward mountains comes from being blown clean off them.

I decided that if the wind knocked me over just once, I'd retreat straight to the escape route. But if I could stay upright I'd stand on top of Meall Mór.

And soon enough, there was the cairn, the unmistakable stack of rocks marking the summit. Due north remained a solid wash of cloud, as did the west, though I could hardly glance that way for the blast of the wind and all its little ice teeth. Otherwise, though, the clouds racing around me were shredding just enough to let through a glimpse here and there of the slopes, though not the summits, of the surrounding mountains.

Despite the blasting cold, I stood a long time on the peak. In summer, people had picnicked there, I was sure. Maybe even made love while the August moon rose over the mountains behind Loch Linnhe. But in January . . . I never wanted to see conditions like this on a mountain again. At least not alone and without proper gear. Such recklessness.

"I'm sorry, Amy and Anya," I whispered as the wind pulled the air from my mouth. And I reminded myself that I wasn't down yet.

I dug in my pack for the peanut butter and jelly sandwiches Amy had fixed me yesterday morning. I ate as I hiked the ridge to the north slope, hoping I'd been right in my reading of the maps and that the going down would be nothing like the going up.

And it wasn't. I had to watch my step, but the wind had blown many patches of ground bare and before long I was down in the grass. I descended through a woods and pasture down to the glen floor, and there was Pigeon, parked right where I'd left her.

Back at the inn, I took a closer look at the day's forecast, pinned to the bulletin board:

> Snow showers and gales over Highlands Scotland; winds as strong as 35–45 mph with gusts over 60; snow showers and blizzards at times; visibility very poor at times, near zero in snow; temperature -2 C and as cold as -17 wind chill; very difficult walking conditions where exposed in higher areas; severe wind chill.

Had I really read that in the morning and let the fair sky outside the door convince me to go up anyway? On the walls around me were framed photos of mountain rescues—a red stretcher basket ascending with a patient toward the belly of a yellow helicopter, a team carrying someone in another such basket down a trail.

I called the cottage.

Anya answered and couldn't wait to tell me she'd been named writer of the day in her class.

"For my story about a trip to Saturn. For our space unit, Daddy. I got a thousand percent on it!"

She'd even made a cardboard and construction-paper figure of the hero, Neil Armstrong.

"In my story he's the first one to make it to Saturn," she explained. "Other people went, but they didn't survive."

"All the braver of him to go," I said. Or foolhardy, I thought to myself.

"You'll be home tomorrow night?" she asked.

"By suppertime."

If this desk didn't overlook the sea, it would be ordinary. If it weren't upstairs in a seventeenth-century cottage and tucked up against a pair of windows, each small pane of which lets in its portion of cloud and sunlight, lobster boats in the tiny harbour, cove beach, and seawall and waves beyond, it would be an ordinary wooden desk. In fact, if Amy and I hadn't carried it up the narrow stairs six months ago for me to use, it wouldn't be a desk at all but just a small dropleaf table beside the sofa down in the low-ceilinged living room. Its dark wood reflects the sky that enters in the shapes of those small window panes. My notepad shares the varnished surface with my few keepsake pebbles, a porcelain creamer with two purple thistles in the slender spout, and the spotting scope through which I sometimes watch the lobster boats coming home through the waves.

This desk is an ordinary thing but for its fortunate place in the world.

Sitting here, I listen to my wife and daughter downstairs, their muffled voices woven with the sighs of waves and a breeze over the chimney and the hiss from a damp, burning log in the fireplace beside me.

How far I've gone for wonder. To feel my life around me as other than ordinary.

I'm a fool, of course. A sucker. The wonderful is always there in the ordinary. Such an old and obvious lesson. It's among the first and last things my mother taught me, one of the most important things I hope to teach my own child in turn. The wonderful is always with you. Just waiting. The only question is what does it take to make you notice.

Today, the muscles in my thighs are tight and my feet are tired. And in that hiss from my fire I hear the sound of snow slipping down a mountain. I hear what might have been the end to all my roaming and seeking, and I slide my hand over the smooth desk and listen to the voices downstairs.

This morning I walked up to the little Crail store for a Sunday newspaper. There at the news rack, in inch-tall black letters, were the words "Three Die in Glen Coe Avalanche." And on the next paper, "Three Killed in Avalanche Horror." And on every other paper, variations of the same headline beside photos of helicopters and rescue vehicles and ambulances and a mountain half-shrouded in cloud.

I picked up one of the papers and read. Three men were dead, killed by a slab of snow that slid over and swept them five hundred feet down the mountain and finally came to rest on top of them. The mountain was Buachaille Etive Mór, just a few summits away from the one I had been climbing at the same time. They had been equipped with ice axes and had been together, climbing an established route. They'd been following the rules. I hadn't.

And here I sit. Watching sunlight now shining on the waves through shifting fissures in the overcast. My daughter and wife downstairs.

Amy sometimes sings the old disco classic "You Sexy Thing" to me when she's feeling playfully amorous. "I believe in miracles," she'll sing and throw me a cute little sideways look so brief it's gone by the time I realize she's done it. A little while ago, after the three of us had finished lunch and cleared the dishes from the table, Amy played the song on the CD player, and she and I danced around the kitchen in each other's arms and Anya rolled her eyes at us. It's the first time Anya's done that in comment on her parents' affection, and I saw in her face a look of half-pleased exasperation I happily supposed we'd be seeing now and then for the next few years.

And it so easily might never have been.

I love this world, especially this Scottish manifestation of it. I love the sea and the companionable mountains and the myth- and muse-haunted glens. But it's not the sea, nor the mountains, nor the glens that love me back. It's the two souls downstairs in this old stone cottage. They, who came all the way over here with me and by doing so made this home, they are the ones who love me back.

"My heart's in the Highlands," Scotland's national poet Robert Burns says. "My heart is not here."

Not so mine. Not today.

Though it's only about half past three and winter solstice is a month behind us, daylight is starting to thin already. If Amy and Anya and I are going to get a stroll down the coast path before dark, we'd better get going.

January 29. My mother's birthday. She would have been sixty-four. As she did, I feel grateful beyond measure for the fifty-nine years of life she got. I celebrate what she had. But I'm sad today too. Sixty-four isn't old. She would have been Anya's young Nana, still. *Will ya still need me, will ya still feed me?* I can hear my mom's voice singing. Would sixty-four really have been so much to ask?

But it doesn't work that way, her voice through the waves outside reminds me. We get what we get. Our job is to make it beautiful.

One summer day she and my dad and my sister and I were sitting in the car out at Presque Isle Park, looking back down the Lake Superior shore at Marquette. From that spot it was and still is hard for me to believe the town—so small from just two miles away, a handful of buildings visible through the trees—was the setting for our great story, was big enough to contain all our fears and suffering and joy and love. And we were just one family. There were twenty-some thousand people in that town, each with a family and stories of fear and suffering, joy and love.

"Almost an Island" Presque Isle means in French. It was our place almost apart, a peninsula, a 323-acre sanctuary from, but still connected to, those Marquette lives we lived. My mother loved to walk the shore and woods of Presque Isle and had done so most summer days before she could no longer walk. It was at Presque Isle that she'd seen Amy and me exchange our wedding vows in a grove of birch at the top of a cliff, that she'd once said in a satisfied voice that she wanted her ashes scattered in the lake one day. And it was there—in that little near-Eden of rocky coast and big old white pines above a forest floor of white trillium—that she stepped on the pebble. Just one sharp little pyramid of a pebble, not even an inch high, that had stuck to the sole of her sneaker. And that, because she'd lost most of the sensation in her feet to diabetes, had burrowed its way in, without her feeling it, with every step she took until it was deep into the flesh of her foot, ending her walking days forever.

Almost an island, *almost* paradise. We take what we get and do all we can to make it beautiful.

The day I remember us sitting in the car looking from Presque Isle downshore at Marquette, my mother had either lost her foot or was staying off it in the hope the ulcer where the pebble had been would finally heal. But she was out in the world anyway, with her adult kids and her husband, eating Togo's submarine sandwiches from the shop near the university. The sounds of our sandwich bags and wax-paper wrappers through the open car window had called down a few curious seagulls who stood in the grass and atop the wooden guardrail beside us. One of the birds with a wing hanging badly askew had walked over to join the wait. We'd be sure to save some nice big pieces of our bread for him.

Then two men walked by, middle-aged guys with buzz cuts and polo shirts. One of them picked up a stone and threw it at the gulls. The man chuckled to his buddy as the birds flew off, all of them except the one with the broken wing. The man picked up another stone.

"Don't you throw that at him!"

The man stopped in his tracks and turned our way, his fist tight on the stone.

"I mean it," my mother warned, looking him dead in the eyes.

The man mumbled something to his buddy and tossed the stone aside. As they walked away he mumbled something else and snorted a loud laugh. I kept my own fists clenched and my eyes on his back until he was out of sight.

It was a very ordinary, small act of courage. Exactly what she believed in. Today, on her birthday, there will be perhaps a billion such acts of courage and decency and kindness in the world. Perhaps two billion. I offer my memory of that one act of my mother's, eight or ten years ago, and of the bread from our Togo's we tossed to that bird, as an example of what one person was. I record it here, for Anya and Amy and whoever else might happen to read this, as my birthday present to my mother. A snapshot, so that it will not be gone from the world.

But then, my mother believed no good act ever perished from the world. Compassion was akin to religion for her, and like the countless prayers offered in any religion, each empathic act, every single moment of courage and decency and kindness on behalf of the weak, mattered and went on mattering because those acts are what sustain the world and our spirits in it.

So I suppose my writing this isn't actually to preserve what my mother did or who she was. Her soul and acts go on, as do all of ours. And it is not to canonize her, for to do that would be to separate her compassion from her ordinary humanity, and she believed compassion was the most ordinary, most human state for any person.

No, I suppose my birthday present to her is not somehow preserving what she did for that wing-broken seagull or putting it into the column of things that count in her favor. Once made, her contribution to the goodness in the world would always be part of the world's ongoing truth. Nobody needs a record keeper for her soul to go on. The present I make to her, here on the page, is not in preserving but simply in remembering, remembering and passing on that memory to others she loved, and maybe here and there to someone she never knew but in whose own capacity for kindness and decency and small acts of courage she would have believed.

Crail is a cold and lonely place today. The sea beyond the seawall is marbled gray and white on the faces of big waves. The constant, hollow sound of wind comes down the chimney and pushes in through the thinnest gaps in the window frames on the other side of this desk.

Yet there's a strange company in the dreariness. It is so much my own state of mind. All day the wind blows and the swells build, a symphony churning up a long constant crescendo to high tide and the last light of day when waves bang into the seawall, shoot thirty or forty feet in the air, blow to mist in the wind that coats my little squares of window panes with a salty film, and fall back down to drench the seawall and run in white rivulets over the old stones and down the worn stone steps and stacks of lobster creels and into the harbour. The little fishing boats pivot and pull and bob against their lines. Light blue and dark blue and yellow and white, they twist restlessly and rock with their orange life preservers stacked two and three between their antennae atop their tiny cockpits.

Out where the horizon would be if the horizon could be seen through the firmament into which the sea disappears, a white light flashes the position of the May Isle lighthouse.

Another wave explodes over the seawall, demolishes itself up into a million sudden fragments, and falls to wash over the fitted rocks and stream over the mortar in the grooves between.

And another wave. And another!

And like any good symphony the storm takes me far from where it had me begin. My dreariness goes, blown and battered into an insistence, a resoluteness, a kind of strength that is part strife, part exuberance, part cleansing grief.

Amy will have a nice fire in the fireplace downstairs. I can smell the garlic and brine of her red clam sauce on the stove. Some of our friends from the village must be here, as expected, for dinner and cards. Through my shut door, I hear Anya and her school chum Emma playing happily in Anya's room across the hall.

Before I go down, I'll click off my desk lamp and sit in the blue near dark and give myself a few more waves shooting up long rows of spray along the seawall.

Amy's good about the birthdays of people in her life. She never lets one go by without some kind of commemoration. January 29, as we were tucking Anya in at the end of the day, Amy suggested we each tell some memories of my mom.

"OK," Anya said and crunched a dry Cheerio, her usual bedtime snack. A snack she and her Nana had shared in bed often.

"I'd like that very much," I said and lay down on one side of Anya while Amy lay down on the other.

"I remember she pushed me the first time I swung in Melissa," Anya started right in. I could picture her, two years old in the blue plastic whale swing in my parents' backyard. My mother was in her wheelchair by then, but she was also out there in the sunshine, wheels in the grass, pushing on Melissa's whale nose every time Anya swung forward, making a wide-eyed face of surprise and joy as if every arrival were a new discovery of her granddaughter.

Two years old would be early to have formed such a memory. We have pictures of that afternoon, though. And whenever we visit that house the same Melissa is out there waiting, a foot of snow on her head sometimes, but always waiting.

I told about watching my mom and Amy give Anya a bath in the kitchen sink. How they bent together over the little baby that forever bonded them, poured warm water from a measuring cup slowly over the wisps of hair on that tiny head.

I told Anya that Nana had to stand the whole time on her one good foot, but she didn't mind. "And they took you out and wrapped you in a towel on the counter. You lay there and Nana leaned down and brought her face very close to your face and your eyes. She spoke very softly and your eyes stared back up at her."

I told it straight, just like that, without commentary. But what I remember now about that kitchen-sink bath of Anya's is the feeling I had, seeing these three generations of women, the love between them in hands touching clean baby skin, and realizing I'd done this. And Amy'd done it too. No matter what else I did or didn't accomplish in my life, I'd fallen in love with her and stuck beside her and we'd brought this baby home to my mother who was now a Nana and the most contented I'd ever seen her.

Amy's memory was next. It was from the same kitchen at my parents' house, two years later at the breakfast table, Nana in her wheelchair and Anya in her lap, the two of them stirring a big enamel bowl of chocolate chip cookie dough.

"Together you'd say, 'mix, mix, mix,' as you stirred," Amy recalled. "I came in and there was flour and sugar all over the table and I said I was sorry about that and Nana said, 'That's OK!' She never minded a mess to clean up. You guys must have finished the batter with an electric mixer because I remember you sitting in her lap later and each of you licking clean a beater, big smiles on your faces."

"I remember," Anya said. Once again I was grateful for the picture Amy had taken, my mom and Anya with big smiles and their cookie-dough beaters. "My turn again," she continued. "I remember sitting in Nana's lap and us rolling in her wheelchair down the ramp into her garden and me asking to do it again and us doing it again."

My next memory was of the kitchen again, but this time looking in. My mom was at the breakfast table where so many times she watched for us to pull into the driveway beside the big kitchen window. And where she'd watch us back out and go, often for months, hundreds of miles of highway away from her. Whether we were coming or going, for months or for hours, she'd wave two hands at us. Big, reaching waves of joy.

"I remember us pulling up and she'd be sitting there, paging through a gardening catalog, thinking about new flowers for the backyard. She'd see our headlights and look up and smile and wave both hands. We'd park and let Yukon out of the truck and he'd make straight for the door, hold his nose right by the doorknob and push his big, heavy body through as soon as I opened it and go straight to my mom. And then you'd toddle in and then my mom would be petting Yukon and holding you and she'd call out, 'The kids are here!' Then my dad would come in from his evening nap on the living room sofa and declare, 'You made it,' and Nana would say, 'They sure did!'"

Anya thought about this scene, half remembering, half reconstructing it, smiled, and yawned. It was about time for us to wish her sweet dreams and pay her the day's last kiss, but Amy had one more memory. This one was from long before Anya was born, from before the Fair Avenue kitchen and backyard, from the days when my family had lived in Marquette only a couple years and were still in our tiny apartment on the campus of Northern Michigan University, where my dad was a new assistant professor. I was a senior at Marquette High School a couple blocks away, and Amy was a junior.

"We were still just friends. We weren't a couple yet," Amy explained. "We used to drive around in my parents' Subaru, sometimes with our friends, but sometimes just the two of us. We'd drive all over town talking. To Presque Isle, to the beach, to Frosty Treats. One day I spilled a milkshake in the car, and I was just panicked."

"You were worried to go home?" Anya asked.

"Yeah, the milkshake was on the seats and all over between them and on the shifter. And Daddy said, 'Let's take it to my mom.' It was the first time I met her. She gathered washcloths and towels and a bucket of soapy water and came out and cleaned it right up, no problem. 'There,' she said kindly to me, 'Good as new.'"

It was the right place to end my mother's birthday, a story of her happy to be able to put things right for someone, the start of the big story of her and Amy's eighteen-year friendship, the first of countless confidences between them.

❦

"The other day, when you told me it was coming up on five years, for a minute I thought that couldn't be right," Amy said as she packed our toiletries, our passports, and her camera into her daypack.

Gray light of morning was coming up over the sea out the window. I slid a fresh yellow legal pad into one of the two small suitcases we'd packed last night.

February 7. The date on the other end of my mother's life, nine days after her birthday. The date of her death. The date that waited on the calendar, all those years, like a pebble on a forest path.

This was the fifth anniversary, and Amy, Anya, and I were going to Paris. It was yet another extravagance we couldn't really afford, but it felt right.

"She would have loved that, Jon," my dad had said on the phone from Michigan when I'd told him our plan.

Amy said so too, in the car as we drove through a light flurry toward the Edinburgh Airport, past snow-filled fields and hedgerows of black and dark-gray trees in relief against the white. "She'd have thought all about us there. She'd have wanted us to tell her everything we planned and wanted to hear every detail when we got back."

It was that thing everyone I've ever known who has lost someone does: say aloud what the one they've lost would have said or felt or done. I've heard it said there's a kind of tyranny in this, a taking of identity from the dead person, who is powerless to be anything but what the living would have them be. Perhaps that's so for some. I can see how it very well could be.

But what's true for me and others I've heard say their dead would have loved or hated or enjoyed or laughed at something is that we don't stop knowing someone when they die. Yes, the world goes on. Unbelievably, idiotically, cruelly, indifferently, gracefully, beautifully, it goes on. And yes, the dead person is left behind. However, when we sense and then say how that person would have reacted to what the new days bring, it's because we still know them. And because we still know them, they still have a relationship to the world that has moved on from their time.

Amy and my dad were right. My mom would have loved the thought of my little family headed off to Paris. She would have lived vicariously in our modest adventure while we were there and would have listened until we were exhausted from telling about it when it was over.

"Today, I'm thinking about what a good listener your Nana was," Amy said to Anya as I drove the winding road through oncoming snowflakes. "Your Nana was a very, very good listener. She'd remember . . ."

Amy was quiet a long time. She didn't continue speaking until she could do so without quavering.

"She'd remember all the details of what people told her, and she'd ask about really specific things later."

It was true. Often, my mother would remember the college class schedules or job prospects or illnesses or vacation plans or daydreams of people with whom she spoke, even casually. She'd recall the names of people she'd never met because those people mattered to the people around her. And she'd ask by name about this teacher or coworker or that relative or friend or romantic interest. She'd remember what the people who spoke to her cared about and hold on to it until their next conversation.

"She and I would just sit and talk for hours and hours," Amy continued. "I really want to be a listener like that for people."

I glanced in the rearview mirror and saw Anya in her booster seat, staring out the window contemplatively.

"She was the kindest person we'll probably ever know," Amy said. "And we know a lot of very kind people," she hastened to add.

I had that particular feeling of comfort one gets when a key personal truth is confirmed by another human being. The enormity of my mother's spirit wasn't something I'd conjured in my mind these last five years. It was so. At least Amy believed it was so, and I trust her more than anyone else to tell me what's real.

"What did I do when she died?" Anya asked.

Amy explained that she and Anya were at her parents' house a half hour away from mine when I called and said Nana had died.

"You had questions. I remember you asked if that meant she was out of breath."

Amy said she gave Anya a choice about coming with her to town and Anya had wanted to, had asked if she could see Nana one more time.

"Was I scared?" Anya asked.

"A little," Amy said. "When you saw she wasn't breathing or moving. But you also wanted to be there."

I remembered. I led Anya into the bedroom. Amy had gone in for her turn alone and was sitting in a chair beside the bed, my mother beside her, propped up with pillows at her back. Two friends, side by side one last time.

Purple blotches were forming on my mother's ears, and though I'd closed her eyes, her mouth hung slightly open.

Anya leaned over onto Amy's lap and kept her gaze fixed on her Nana. Amy stroked Anya's hair.

On we drove into the present day.

"Do you know what an obituary is?" Amy asked.

"No," Anya said.

Amy explained the term and told Anya that I'd sat down and written Nana's that same afternoon, all about her life and the people she loved.

"Was I in it?" Anya asked.

"Of course," I said. "You were the arrival. You were the new person, the next piece of our family. The best thing about the last years of her life was you."

Amy went on to tell how we all—she and Anya, my dad and sister, my mother's sister and brother, and I—had gone to Vango's Pizza on Third Street for lunch.

To myself I recalled that we'd left so as to be gone when the undertaker came to the house with his long black car and wheeled my mother forever away from her home and snowed-over garden.

Later, when I spoke to him in his office in the funeral home I was struck by how young the undertaker seemed in his crisp shirt and suit, his hair cut to a buzz above his ears. He was much younger than me. My mom would have liked that, I recalled thinking. She was a champion of those just starting off, sympathetic to their need to prove themselves and find a place in the world. It was the first time I thought how she would have felt about something in the world she did not know.

Amy told Anya how the sun came out the day my mother died and the rest of us all drove out to the rocky Lake Superior shore at Presque Isle. A few hours of spring in the midst of winter. We parked at the log pavilion where we'd had Anya's first birthday, just above the paved path along which I'd pushed my mother in her wheelchair, Anya in her lap, into the summer wind off the lake and the seagulls holding the air around them.

"She loved seagulls?" Anya said in her half-question, half-statement inflection.

"That's right," I said. "She certainly did."

Our plane rose from the Scottish snow up into the sunshine, but it was snowing again as we made our descent. Anya polished off her Air France hot chocolate and declared it "one of the best hot chocolates in the world." It was the first detail of our trip I'd have told my mom. And they continued to add up. As we taxied toward the terminal the captain welcomed us to Paris in French and again in English. Vivaldi came softly on the PA. *No lack for flair, the French*, I'd have told her.

I'd been worried that Anya would be worn out by the day's travel and our talk of her Nana's death. To my surprise, though, she was giddy to be in Paris. Normally, she merely tolerates eating out and, finicky eater that she is, often rejects her food after one bite with a guilty shrug and a meek "sorry" as soon as the waiter is out of sight. But at the first taste of her first Parisian meal, a simple poached salmon, she went wide-eyed and said, "It's the best salmon in the world! Every bite is a little bit of heaven." And a short time later she discovered that, like Air France's hot chocolate and her first French salmon, her first French chocolate mousse was quite to her liking.

Our lean, jovial waiter checked in on us and smiled. "She's the princess, yes?"

"Ah, yes," I confessed. "The princess."

From the restaurant we rushed to Pont Neuf on the Seine to make an 8:00 p.m. boat cruise. Anya led the way and tugged on our hands as we ran.

Amy and I were in Paris the summer I was twenty and she was nineteen. We'd taken a night cruise down the river then, sitting atop the tour boat with our cheese and bread and bottle of wine. Amy showed the photos to my mom when we got home. Now, twenty-one years later we had an eight-year-old with us, an eight-year-old who could not have been more pleased to be there, among the few people braving the open seats atop this tour boat in the chilly night air.

"Take a picture of me in front of it!" she told Amy when the highest twinkling lights and spinning beacon atop the Eiffel Tower came into view. And she asked Amy to keep taking photos as it got closer.

When we were right alongside it, I pointed up to the restaurant on the first level above the four iron legs and said, "Your mom and I had dinner there."

I recalled us splurging, me plunking down my first credit card because we'd burned through most of the few hundred in cash we'd worked all year to save for that summer. Our Eiffel Tower meal and the rest of our days wandering around Europe weren't paid off for several years, and here we were at it again, spending into the red to live it up again. Gathering stories.

Later, we were up in Montmartre, amid the winding, narrow streets to take in the rooftop night views from that hilly Paris district, when I saw them—a couple about twenty ascending the stairs from the metro, an overstuffed backpack weighing him down, a duffel slung protectively across her front. She had a guidebook in one hand. They looked disoriented and bushed but excited to finally be near wherever it was they were headed.

There we were, Amy and me, those two decades ago. I wished them well. As well as us. And I hoped that when they were two decades older they, like us, wouldn't trade places with their former selves, as happy as they'd been back then.

The rest of my little family is asleep now, my wife and daughter. I'm up late at the desk in our hotel room, writing in the soft light from the window.

Every detail we wanted to tell. That's what my mom would have wanted to hear. So I'm telling those details anyway. Telling them to Anya if she's reading this one day. Telling them to the cold Paris night outside. Telling them to you.

I'm reluctant to let the day end. To leave the fifth year without my mother and begin the sixth. But we go on, into the life my mother did not know. The life into which she wished us.

Through an off-again-on-again rain, Amy, Anya, and I walked a tree-lined sidewalk above the Seine. Our stroll led us to a little row of pet shops, and at Anya's eager suggestion, we crossed the street to investigate. Though she had expressed a reasonable interest in what I'd told her would be our destination—Notre Dame, with its gargoyles and vast, dark interior and story of the Hunchback—she was far more amused by the kittens, puppies, hamsters, and mice in the windows. At the third pet shop we came to Amy and I finally relented and agreed that yes, all right, we could go in for a few minutes. Notre Dame would wait.

As we moved from cage to cage we saw Chihuahuas for €2800, Persian cats for €1800. Garden-variety kittens like the ones kids give away from cardboard boxes in front of American grocery stores were €850. Hamsters were €80! As I looked out the pet-shop window and down the river at the thirteenth-century building in which Marie Antoinette awaited execution, it occurred to me that, despite the most drastic of efforts to stamp it out, decadence is perennial.

But Anya had been too busy flitting from cage to cage, pointing out this then that cute little being, to notice the price cards. When we stepped back outside and walked on she was lit up, talking with hardly a pause for breath about the turtle and hamster we promised she could have when we return home next August. She's a good sport about all this wandering her parents are putting her through, our own decadence, I suppose.

Later, after the darkness and candles and vaulting stone pillars of Notre Dame, she got herself up for the Louvre and our usual game of "pick the postcards from the gift shop and find the artwork." I was concerned about how it'd go. With eighteen miles of exhibits, the Louvre is the largest art museum in the world. But we'd unfolded the map, located the ancient-Egyptian halls, and set off to find the first work, a little (of course our first goal would have to be little) blue ceramic hippopotamus.

It took a while. Room after room of sarcophagi, pots, and sphinxes passed, but Anya showed no signs of flagging. Finally, when I was all but sure that we must have passed it somewhere in the scores of display cases, Anya exclaimed, "There it is!"

She held the postcard up to the glass cabinet, and, sure enough, there was the little blue hippo: "Hippopotamus figurine. 1650–1550 BCE."

We played our seek-and-find game for several more hours as rain poured on the courtyards and glass pyramids out the tall windows, then Anya spent her own euros back at the gift shop on a four-inch plush version of the blue Egyptian hippo, a new friend for her constant bedtime companion, Little Lamb.

Amy and I are usually pretty good about knowing and respecting Anya's limits, and one a day is certainly her limit for museums. But the rain was still coming down, so we headed over to see the modern art in the Pompidou Centre where we'd be dry. It went OK for a while. We stood in front of some Baques and Légers, and I gave Anya my teacherly two cents on Cubism—the artist presenting multiple views at once and thereby escaping the constraints of time.

"More about ideas than feelings, really," I admitted. "But I like it anyway."

"Me too," she said, though I was unsure if earnestly or dutifully. Her earnestness was unmistakable, though, when she asked hopefully, "Can we go now?"

"Soon," I told her. I was shot myself, tired to the point of tremulous and bleary. Amy and I just wanted her to see the Warhols and Magrittes before we left. "Soon," we promised.

But after we'd seen the rest of the Pompidou's permanent collection, it was the famed view from the top floor we had to take in before going.

"Look at that!" I said as the Eiffel Tower's beacon spun along the bottom of the cloud ceiling. "And see Notre Dame where we were this morning?"

Amy clicked photos through the rain-splattered glass.

When Anya turned from the view to me, I saw the tear rolling down her cheek.

"Oh, Baby," I said.

"Anya?" Amy lowered her camera. "Oh, Sweetie," she put her arm around Anya. "We wore you out, didn't we?"

"I just want to get back to the hotel," she said quietly.

"Of course we can," I told her.

"Of course, Baby," Amy said.

The rain let up as we walked. We bought pizzas and fruit and bread along the way, went back to the room, crawled under the covers, and watched *Nim's Island* on Amy's laptop. On the nightstand beside Anya was a little ten-euro Eiffel Tower she'd bought from a street vendor. The Egyptian hippo—Bluey, as Anya had named her—rested snugly under Anya's arm with Little Lamb.

If I could send my mother a postcard, I would tell her Anya has discovered she loves croissants. I would tell her how we bought three for breakfast from a tiny bakery and ate them from the paper sacks as we strolled vaguely through a drizzle toward the river. And I would tell her how we crossed over to the Left Bank and found Shakespeare and Company bookstore, the center of the English-speaking expatriate literary community in Paris for eighty-nine years.

I wonder if my mom knew about the bookstore. As a literature scholar, she likely did. In its two previous Left Bank locations Shakespeare and Company was frequented by writers like Hemingway, Pound, Fitzgerald, and Stein. Sylvia Beach, the store's founder, published the first edition of Joyce's *Ulysses.* The store's current location, across the Seine from Notre Dame Square, was a haunt of Ginsberg and Burroughs and now hosts another generation of young expat writers who exchange a few hours of work for lodging in bunks tucked among the upstairs bookshelves.

If I could send her a postcard, I'd tell my mom the bookstore was crowded in every corner and to the beamed ceiling with its own history. A keyboard emerged from between a stack of books on the floor and books on what I realized were a piano's lid. Wood chairs and stools—no two alike but all with layers of old, cracked paint—stood on the thread-worn carpets and bare stone floor in the narrow corridors and nooks. Even the stone ring of what had once been a well in the floor was topped with stacks of books. Coins dotted the cement three feet down where the well had been filled in. Handbills for writers' groups and readings competed for space on the door, windows, and several bulletin boards. The scent of incense and clatter of a typewriter drifted down the steps. A black dog tugged playfully on a young woman's glove, refusing to let go.

"Sorry, she does that a lot," the young woman behind the counter said in an Australian accent.

It was impossible to take it all in at once. For me anyway. But Anya squeezed right past and headed up the stairs, between stacks of books on every tread, following the signs to the children's section. Amy subtly lifted her camera to her eye.

In my daze I found the handwritten "Poet's Corner" sign and spent a few minutes at the shelves there, scanning the spines for poets with Paris roots. Soon I had a little stack of books that included Apollinaire, Celan, Rimbaud, Valéry, and Villon. With the stack under my arm I followed Anya upstairs, toward the sources of the typewriter clatter and incense, and found her engaged in conversation with an elderly lady. The woman thanked her in a French accent for her help and explained to me that Anya had been assisting her in selecting a book for her English granddaughter.

If I could send my mom a postcard, I'd tell her how Anya said, "You're welcome," cheerfully, how the elderly woman paid her an "au revoir" and made her way carefully down between the books on the stairs, how Anya said, "I've got a stack, too, Daddy!" and showed me her books.

If I could, I'd tell my mom about spotting the typist—a long-haired, bearded young man working away at the machine between a smoldering incense stick and a steaming cup of coffee—as Anya and I made our way through a sitting room and down a narrow hall walled in more bookshelves with curtained-off bunks here and there for young writers, through a doorway above which were painted the words "Be not inhospitable to strangers lest they be angels in disguise," and into a room lined with cushioned benches and still more bookshelves.

Amy joined us, and I asked if she was taking some good photos.

"I think so. And I found a book." She handed me the novel *Hunting and Gathering* by Anna Gavalda, a story of Parisian misfits, the cover explained. Amy has a huge soft spot for misfits, wherever they may be. Lucky for me.

I sat in one of the chairs at the window overlooking rue de la Bûcherie, the Seine, and Notre Dame Square beyond. Cozied up next to a portable radiator I scribbled in my pocket notebook and glanced now and then out at the streets, wet with rain again.

Amy took my picture. It's good to have a partner who sees you as you enjoy imagining yourself. I'm not a renowned writer. My books weren't downstairs on one of the shelves in Poet's Corner. But that was all right. My daughter was sitting across the room, paging through her illustrated Roman mythology, my wife was documenting our Paris afternoon with her camera, and I was doing so with my pen. The three of us were composing our own story. We were our own audience.

That picture is the postcard I would send, if I could, to my mom.

In the morning on the train to the airport an accordion player strolled into our car. He was playing "Those Were the Days." Decades before it was popularized in America in the sixties—my mother's golden youth—it was a Russian song, and as the accordionist weaved and staggered toward us through the rocking train, the song seemed to come from generations of people who were once young. Notice, the accordion was telling us. Notice your life, the days passing each into the next like these notes.

When he was done I put a couple brass-colored euro coins in the Styrofoam cup he held as he passed on his way to the next car. I stared out the window. Scrapyards and gray housing projects of the Paris suburbs passed.

In her youth my mother had daydreamed of directing films. I let myself imagine the accordionist's song still playing in my head as her choice for this moment, as the romantic, already nostalgic accompaniment to the end of our four days in Paris.

I cannot tell her about our little adventure, cannot give it to her for her to make of it a pleasant vision in her mind. But she would have loved it. And because I know she would have loved it, she can still remind me to notice, to be inside these days and, as the song says, to live the life we choose.

Marquette, Day Four

February 5 . . .

Cleaned Mom's raw bedsores at six this morning. The key is to be methodical and smooth. To get through the pain as gently and quickly as possible but to be deliberate with the swabbing and applying the fresh, soft moleskin dressing.

Even so she winced and her forehead creased with the hurt of our work.

To keep the mood up, Ann and I sang "Under the Boardwalk," a favorite of Mom's.

It was a bit jumbled, but when I forgot some lyrics, I substituted, "Sheila, down by the Santa Monica Pe-e-eir."

We worked delicately but fast.

Ann and I sang.

Dad backed us with the refrain, "Under the boardwalk . . ."

And together the three of us repeated, "Boardwalk."

Softly but clearly we sang, "On a blanket with my baby is where I'll be . . ."

Then we sang "California Girls," which made Dad tear up.

When the bedsores were clean under fresh, smooth moleskin, Mom managed a few sips of orange electrolyte drink. We wetted her eyes with artificial teardrops, tucked her back under the covers, and sat around her on the bed until she was sleeping sweetly.

Later in the morning, when Mom was awake again, she'd had some time when she seemed present, so I used it to say, "We're doing OK. Ann and Dad and I are getting through this. We're going to take care of each other and get through it."

She'd opened her eyes and looked into mine—tiny pupils again, narrow openings between lids—and said completely clearly, "There will be times."

Always thinking of us.

I'd said, "How about during those times you come and be with us?"

People visit. Rick, my college friend, has brought his little boy Ricky to show him to Mom. When Rick and I were young men, Mom and Rick connected as fellow "lost family" people. Rick was on his own then, an exile, if not an outright orphan like her. She made him welcome, listened to him talk about classes, girls, loneliness.

Now he's driven nine hours to show her his little son.

He calls her the most wonderful person he knows.

Others gather. My mom's brother and sister are here from far away to sit with her and stroke her hair and look at old family photos. My mom's sister-in-law has made the long journey too. Amy's sister comes by.

And Amy is here. Mom's dear, dear friend and daughter-in-law.

And Anya, the grandchild we gave her.

The house fills with conversation. Life. Anya "reads" three or four books to her. She sits in my lap beside her and goes through the stuff she has memorized. When she's done she asks Mom if she liked it, and Mom nods yes.

At one point today, when we were alone, I told Mom I was going to keep talking to her, going to keep her going in me.

Her face was pained.

I asked her if she wanted me to stop, if it hurt too much.

"No," she said, though she looked so sad.

I told her I'd seen a heavy man walking across campus today. I said that while most people who would drive by wouldn't pay him much thought or would think, "There's a heavy guy" or worse, she *would think, "It must be hard to be in there. I hope he has some joy in his day, someone who cares about him."*

She nodded.

I told her I would live to keep her compassion going.

Tonight, after she fell asleep, I spent an hour cleaning her rump, trimming and replacing the soiled parts of the bedsore dressings. Because she was unconscious and seemed not to feel it, I took the time to work meticulously, cleaning and rinsing with Q-tips.

Now comes an odd sense of happiness to have done that.

I hope she sleeps through the night. For her and me.

Scotland, Late Winter and Early Spring

Back from Paris, we soon found our cottage turning into a cave around us. We made efforts to keep it from happening. We woke one morning to a real snowfall, a rarity in Crail, and went out and built two snowmen—one in front of our door and another out on the breakwater. Amy took photos of the wet snow piled on the lobster creels and gunwales of boats. We built a snow fort on the seawall, and Anya crawled in, and we all threw snowballs at one another.

Our two snowmen stared at each other across the harbour for a few days as the temperature climbed and the sun broke out. But soon they, and the little snow fort on the seawall, were smears of white, and then they were gone.

The sun traded places with clouds and mist. One morning we'd hear the small songs of returning birds through our curtains and single-pane windows. The next morning we'd hear nothing but waves and battering wind.

We got the flu. For three weeks fever, chills, and cramps kept one of us under the covers and the other two in attendance and semihousebound.

The worst of the winter darkness was subsiding. Daylight was lingering until five now, rather than winking out at three thirty, but as the days of February dragged by, I became more and more aware that the walls around us were thick, cold stone.

All three of us checked out on Scotland mentally. I began to daydream about someday buying a house in Marquette, and Amy browsed realty sites online. She wrote daily e-mails and made late-night calls to friends across the ocean. Anya got out library books on raising gerbils and explained to us that when we get back home she'll need to get more than one. Otherwise they get lonely, she explained. One alone will try to dig right through the woodchips of its cage to find others.

And were Amy and I imagining it, or did we notice that Anya seemed to be spending time alone in the schoolyard before the morning bell? Were her friends grouping up with other kids and excluding her?

While the other parents attempted to make idle chat with us, we stood in the drizzle at the school gate and kept our eyes on Anya's red jacket, which seemed to move from cluster to cluster and kept ending up alone. After the bell rang and kids went inside, we would go back to the cottage where Amy would cry and ask what had gone wrong.

"Maybe her friends are starting to realize she'll be leaving in five months," I guessed. "I don't know. It was going so well for her. I don't get it."

Amy wondered if Anya's tendency to form one or two close friendships had backfired on her. Or maybe it was her affectionate nature, and other kids were cutting her off—as kids will—just because they could. Amy lost a lot of sleep.

But we kept trying. We read Harry Potter aloud every night. We played cards and dice and Clue. We held hands around the dinner table and took turns telling what we were grateful for—each other, our returning health, our cottage, the steaming salmon and rice and carrots on our plates. We really tried.

But then Anya would ask if we'd mind too much if she played one of her computer games before bed, and Amy and I would welcome the chance to plop down on the sofa and numb out in front of some BBC drama on TV. And then I'd ask myself again what the point in coming here had been, as the walls around us once again insisted on their stones, and the curtains and door on the front of our cave stayed tightly shut to the indifferent lighthouse pulsing out on the indifferent sea.

To what extent Anya's recent social difficulties result from her foreignness, I haven't been able to ascertain, but even as she keeps trying, her troubles go on. Yesterday, she invited over Lilly and Emma, her two best friends from her class, for pizza and milkshakes and a movie. Amy and I had suggested the get-together after Anya told us she was feeling excluded, even from those kids to whom she had, until recently, felt closest. The three girls were in Anya's room while Amy was downstairs making the shakes, and I heard Lilly's and Emma's voices and the sound of Anya's crying.

I tapped on the open door and saw Lilly and Emma on one side of the bed and Anya on the far side, tears welling in her eyes.

"What's going on?" I asked.

Anya's tears ran down her cheeks, and Lilly giggled nervously.

I put my arm around Anya. "She's crying and you're giggling?" I asked sharply.

Anya couldn't bring herself to say anything, but Emma and Lilly fell all over each other to explain that Anya hadn't helped them with the team challenge that day at school.

"So you're making her cry?" Then I pulled out the big ammo. Things they didn't know I knew. "Lilly, I've heard that groups of girls at school have excluded you lately. And Emma, didn't Abbey and Ellie make you cry at school a couple days ago?"

The girls nodded, relieved to be painted as fellow victims rather than perpetrators.

"Well, I think it's pretty disappointing that the three of *you* can't be good to one another, can't stick together and be kind." I asked if I should take them home, and Anya shook her head no vigorously and looked pleadingly into my eyes.

"No, no," Lilly said.

"We're the BFF Club," Emma said.

"Best friends forever," Lilly insisted.

"Well, kindness only in our house is the rule," I said and retreated, leaving the door ajar.

Two minutes later I heard them all giggling and wrestling on the bed. But then, once the movie was started there was a squabble because Lilly wanted Emma to sit in the middle. And then again this morning in the schoolyard Anya seemed to spend the long minutes before the first bell alone.

The sun is out today. I ran the shore path, past the ruined cottage and alongside waves tossing over the rocks as B. B. King sang "The Thrill Is Gone" in my headphones. I came home and sat beside Amy on the couch, and we talked about Anya's troubles until we'd said everything we could think to say: maybe she should just be homeschooled for the remainder of our time here; or maybe that would be the worst thing for her confidence and skills, especially given how much she seems to be enjoying her academic activity, currently a report on Pluto she's happily researching; maybe her friends are pulling back because they realize she'll be leaving; maybe the intensity of Anya's affection and loyalty has put them off; maybe it's us and how much time she spends with us and other adults; maybe she's actually more socially advanced (she seems to get on consistently well with kids a couple years older than herself); maybe she lets her need show and thereby has driven kids away.

I want to call my mom, to hear her voice reassuring me from Marquette as it did through my first nearly four years of being Anya's dad. I try, but today I cannot conjure what my mom would have said.

The songbirds have returned; I can hear them this morning on the roof.

Anya's still feeling disconnected from the girls in her grade, but she invited over Alice and Marion, "the twins," for a play date. They are two years older than Anya and big fans of Harry Potter. The three got on wonderfully. They made a fort of the couch, chairs, and blankets in the living room and crawled in with head lamps on their heads.

Amy went to see Mrs. Laing, Anya's teacher, and spoke with her about the isolation Anya's been telling us about. Supportive and encouraging as ever, Mrs. Laing said that Anya continues to do well in her studies, but there has been a noticeable dip in her social confidence. She said she'd keep an eye out for ways she could help, that she'd be rearranging the class seating, and she'll put Anya with some kids who seem particularly warm.

Of course Amy's still concerned, but she's stopped weeping daily. To make things even brighter, our first of many scheduled spring visitors has arrived with the songbirds. A friend and former student of mine, Jaime is a long-haired, flannel-clad, Seattle bohemian who is also so conscientious and responsible that Amy and I trusted him to be Anya's first babysitter. But what I love most about Jaime is his largeness of heart. His kindness and interpersonal attentiveness make him one of what I think of as my mother's people, those rare individuals one meets every year or two—if one is lucky enough—whose very core is compassion, for whom the well-being and contentment of others is their deepest motivator and concern. They are a tribe, dispersed across time and geography, but they are easily recognized by those of us who have loved one of them.

Jaime, Amy, Anya, and I drive through the Highlands and over the bridge to the Isle of Skye. In the Pier Restaurant in the village of Portree we are the first customers of the spring season. We sit beside the window with the full moon on the fishing boats at anchor. When, for conversation, I ask everyone what personal quality they'd most like to have more of, Jaime answers, "Grace."

Grace. Of course. Who besides those who already have it could think to want more, above all other qualities? Jaime tells me I was a good teacher for him. But it's Jaime who teaches me now. Though he never met her, his word teaches me what my mother's people wish for when they wish for themselves.

A turn in the tide for Anya. Maybe. Emma and Lilly each invite her for play dates. She turns them down; she tells us she'd rather be home playing with Amy and me.

"Everything's going OK, though?" we ask, and she tells us yeah. All the kids are being nice to her again. Emma and Lilly have told her they really want to be friends. And she's once again in a bright mood when we pick her up, eager to tell us what's new. Today it's a sticker on her uniform sweatshirt for playing a good game of cricket. She skips toward home as she tries to explain the rules to me.

Still, much as things seem to be improving in her social life, she'd rather spend her free time with us instead of other kids in the village. Once bitten, twice shy it seems.

It's OK, I suppose, her choosing her family over friends right now.

The sun's come out, and mid-March feels like much-later spring. I think I'll suggest we take a picnic out to the shore.

More company from across the Atlantic. For the three years before we moved to Scotland, Cousin Jennifer lived in our house while attending college and was like a sister to Anya. It was Jennifer who introduced Anya to Harry Potter, Jennifer with whom Anya first climbed our backyard trees. She has an unfailingly cheerful disposition, and having her here makes Scotland feel a little more like home.

Jennifer shared her flight over with some of our beloved family friends who have come to visit for a week. And so we've re-created our American household in our Crail cottage: the adults putting the pajama-clad little people to bed, and then back to bed, and then back to bed one last time; Amy the next morning teasing Jennifer she's slept late so there's no hot water left; and Jennifer half believing her when in fact the tank's long since recovered from the early risers' bathing and breakfast dishes.

At the moment, Amy, Anya, Jennifer, and our friends from home are down on the beach, and I'm alone with my window onto the sea and my pen and paper. In her last years, my mom spent her share of time alone, her husband off in his professor role in front of class, her son on one side of the country, and her daughter on the other, the upper Michigan night out her window. She often told me she was grateful for this solitary time.

I suppose solitude is how some of us perfect our love for one another—me here at my desk while my little congregation plays downshore, my mom in her wheelchair at the dining room table and looking out into a dark blizzard through which the strongest affection and the best of good wishes traveled easily.

Mothering Sunday. The third Sunday of March in the UK. We're back in the Highlands, back at Glenfinnan House Hotel, this old manor of high ceilings, flickering candles, and oil paintings on the shore of my mother's near namesake loch, Loch Shiel. When we asked our friend Chris what she and her kids would like to see in Scotland and she answered the Highlands, I jumped at the chance to stay here again. So I'm up late writing once again in this wing-back chair next to the fire in the lobby fireplace.

It seems odd to me, of course, to have Mothering Sunday come so early compared to the American Mother's Day in May. Odd, but fitting. Today the daffodils were up; the songbirds were back. We saw four early lambs in fields on the drive up from Crail. The world is on the brink of remaking itself, of handing down life to a new generation. Once we had checked into the hotel I celebrated the day with my mother by speaking to her as I ran eighteen miles of dirt road alongside the wild loch she never saw, never even heard of, as far as I know, but that her son has come to love through eyes trained to the world's companionability by her. She was here, in the wind and clouds and rain and sunlight moving between the steep slopes rising from the loch, because *I* was here.

As I ran I told her how Anya's getting on, that February was tough, but it's three weeks behind us, and today's a new day. The wind and rain sculpted my jacket to the contours of my body, and I told her that I've made peace, for now anyway, with losing the audience I imagined my Keats and Fanny film would have found. That I've made peace generally with my work's lack of audience. "I don't need to be famous," I said. "The work makes my soul larger, sustains it at least. In turn I'm better able to love your sweet friend and daughter-in-law, and your Little Sprite, the one who made you

Nana and who, God willing, will carry both your spirit and mine on in the world."

The loch moved rows of white waves like choral voices over its blue-black depths. The low sky was darkening. It would be night soon. My feet moved over the packed dirt road. I jumped puddles.

"They're back there." I nodded up the loch. Soon I'd be able to see the lights of the hotel through the dusk and gauzes of rain moving just above the water. "Thank you," I said. "For this life, for my feeling so alive in it. And for teaching me to love."

And then it came to me, clear as if her voice were speaking.

With them is where I find her most.

Ever since she died it has seemed that there should be somewhere I could go to find her. Scotland. The seaside. This loch. The cottage in which her beloved Wordsworth lived. The hills he walked. Her Marquette dining room table where she sat alone looking out the picture window at the dark and loving us out there. So often I've felt this overwhelming sense that if I could just find the right place, I'd find her.

"But it's with them," I said through my hard breaths as I ran. "That's where you are, where you've been all along. Where you'll remain."

Now, as I write this, the logs in the fire are glowing, crumbled orange blocks that send up flickers of flame. From the pub down the hall there's fiddle music, the sound of glasses being washed and shelved. The gusting wind puffs billows of smoke up in front of the mantel once in a while and rattles across the tall dark window.

And home is my family and dear friends, asleep upstairs.

Crail. Daffodils along dry-stone walls, up steep braes, yellow in the wind. Morning silhouette of a lone figure in an outboard skiff writing a silver V of sun on the blue-and-silver sea. Dove voice down the chimney. Translucence of a tilting gull's wing. A single filament of spider web shining in the corner window pane. Spotty bright film of dry brine from the spray of a storm last winter on the glass. Floating gulls that turn like little swans in the shimmer pattern of breeze through the harbour. Dry rope of creels stacked on the pier and on boats. Wet rope of slack tie lines where they curve through the surface. Pale-to-white-green lichen and deep-green moss on the garden wall's rock. Ten million colors the human eye can read while it lives and every color sun. The first lambs are somewhere in the hills, and the hills are sprouting grass.

Like no place else I know, Scotland can turn mournful to wondrous as swiftly and truly as the human heart. The sky will be low and close, the sea a gray that insists it will outlast you, the slopes shrouded in mist, the skin of every woebegone thing wet, everything elegy. And then at evening the clouds will move and shred in layers of altitude, will open but close again, disassembling whatever sky's above until finally giving over to let in the gloaming and then the stars. Then morning will rise on a coast so bright it's as if nothing ever need die.

It's an ancient fallacy to say so, I know, but Scotland seems to understand.

March ends today. Guests go, our friend Chris and her children back to home and work and school in America, and guests come, Amy's folks again with grandparent hugs for Anya and stories of three hundred inches of snowfall (so far) and three feet of ice on the lake at their secluded log home near Marquette. Meanwhile more daffodils than I ever knew existed bloom in the Scottish sun, every one of them an ambassador from where my mother has gone.

If I could film any ten seconds of this life and somehow send those ten seconds to my mother, these might well be them. Anya is on a blond horse. Her ponytail bobs up and down and blows in the wind as the horse trots and wind blows across its tail and blond mane. Girl and horse cross the newly green field in front of the farm just outside Crail where Anya takes riding lessons. Up one side of the field, a row of centuries-old maples, still winter bare. Up the opposite side, another row of centuries-old maples, also still winter bare but with daffodils speckled beneath. Out beyond the field and stone fences, the open sea and the Isle of May. Here, where I watch in front of the old stone farmhouse, more daffodils, more daffodils than I have ever seen in one place, thousands of them tilting and leaning with the spring breeze.

If I could, I would show my mother ten seconds of this so she could see her one grandchild this confident on her saddle, in the world, with herself, surrounded by so much beauty, a moving painting in the leaning light when afternoon turns to evening. And then, when Anya has ridden over to her instructor Alice at the fence and I think this moment I would send is complete, I hear Alice ask Anya if she's ever ridden bareback.

"Not here," Anya says as an involuntary grin spreads across her face.

Anya climbs down, Alice removes the saddle, boosts Anya back up, and Anya and horse walk back out into my mother's dream.

Spring is Scotland's most insistent season, and what the spring in Scotland insists on is now. Grass grows among the ruins. This year's lambs call out and kick and scurry as the only lambs the world will ever know (never mind the stone fence around the pasture and the netherworld from which it came). Every place grows from its own remains, but nowhere else I've been seems so indifferent in its growing from such enduring remains.

Do we call this time Easter and see resurrection in it because we could never stand to see the way the new is *not* the old recovered, but in fact obliterates the old?

The fledgling leaves of a little urban elm reflecting up off the hood of a Mini Cooper parked at the curb next to my St. Andrews café table have never been before. Sure, the tree itself comes back into green. But never the leaves. That boy who toddles by holding some big person's hand and gives me a passing glance is no other boy who has ever been. He is completely new and all of history's children before him are nowhere to be seen today. Today is his.

So how does one mourn in a spring like Scotland's spring? Where does one find the dead?

One doesn't. They aren't out there, among the gulls and waves, the new children and leaves, the tweed-coated scholars studying at their chrome café tables in the sun. In the spring, one mourns not by seeking the dead, but by thanking them.

This is the world into which our dead wished us, a kind of afterlife not for them but for us. And as is so obvious along the cobblestone lanes and ancient sheep fields and flowering ruins of Scotland, it is the way of the world that this new day is possible, this new life has a chance, only because the old has gone and made way. Regretlessly, like my mother, or otherwise, the dead have gone just the same. And we may consider that a gesture on their part, for if their days never went, this day would never have come. For these children to feel the sun on their faces, each child who came before has given up the sun.

Spring is Scotland's most insistent season, and it insists on now. Scotland does not insist that we feel gratitude for those who gave us this moment, that we even pay them a passing thought as we sit in today's sun. But by doing so, I feel the sun as that much warmer and see these new little leaves as that much more intricate and fine. I thank my mother, and all the children who had their days once, for that passing boy's face.

Amy's folks have gone back to Michigan once again, but my cousin Jennifer will be staying a while longer. In the morning as I write at my desk by the window I can often hear her and Anya through the door, playing roles and making up scenarios.

"Tonks!" I just heard Jennifer admonish. "We can't let the muggles see you like this, a purple cheetah!"

Anya replied with high-pitched cheetah squeaks of happy unconcern.

At dusk Jennifer often goes out walking the coast path and gathering driftwood in sacks, the wind in over the waves across her long, curly, yellow hair. She comes home and builds the evening fire with her finds, then sits up close to the fireplace, warming her hands as the salty wood snaps with silver sparks, crackles, and burns bright gold.

Last night the rest of us joined her on her driftwood walk. We got as far as the ruined cottage before we turned back with our sacks full and the daylight all but drained from the air around us. At home Jennifer built the fire. We all played a quick game of cards then took turns reading Harry Potter aloud.

As we tucked Anya into bed, it occurred to me that Jennifer and Anya are only a dozen years apart in age. One day (God willing, a long time from now), after Amy and I are gone, Anya will have Jennifer to remember Crail with, to remember gathering driftwood out by the ruined cottage in the dusk, as gulls turned and waves spilled over the rocks and rattled the stones on the beach, to remember saying goodnight to the lighthouse out the window and the sound of those waves outside in the dark as we read Harry Potter and the cottage filled with the homey smell of salty wood crackling in the fireplace.

Notice April. Notice everything about April you can. I tell myself this in our garden, which slopes up the hill behind our cottage to a weathered picnic table at which I sit in the sun and look out over our mossy tiled roof and the harbour and sea beyond. New leaves and new blooms surround me. The smell of roses. The cheeping and cawing and peeping and twittering of birds comes from seven different directions when I close my eyes and count. The sea is calm. The slosh of the littlest of waves on the reef and seawall drifts up to me.

Is this the destination, then?

Yesterday, as Jennifer and I drove back from a marathon I'd run in the Highlands, we debated the question of whether the point of life is really the journey (my position) or the destination (her position). We often make a game of arguing such inane questions, and she generally enjoys taking the side contrary to whatever homespun wisdom is up for discussion. She's such a wise and patient young person, it's amusing to hear her take contrary or cynical positions. She knows this, of course, and enjoys the effect.

"Think about it," she said as the dark mountains sloped around us in the dusk and our headlights followed the curving road along rock walls and through overhanging tree limbs. "If living was all about the journey, nobody'd ever get anything done. Everyone'd just, you know, keep moving with no point."

There is nobody I know less concerned with getting to the point and more contented to enjoy the moving than Jennifer. It's part of what makes her such great company. She delights, just about every day, in simply seeing what that day brings. But I played along and did my best to argue her out of her put-on cynicism.

"Think about a good marriage," I said. "In a good marriage there's no end point in the future toward which you're striving, no finish line when things will be right. At least there shouldn't be. A good marriage is about every day."

"Then that's the goal, isn't it? That's the destination."

"Now you're just talking semantics."

"No," she said as if aghast at the inference. "I'm not. If you have a goal that things will be good every day in a marriage—say, when you get married—and then things are good, you're at your destination."

"Undergrads," I said, exasperated.

"Old people."

"Old people?"

"Sorry. I couldn't think of anything else fast enough. Don't worry, though, people are living a lot longer nowadays."

Now, sitting amid seven directions of birdsong in the garden, the sun warming my shoulders, I wonder if Jennifer may have had a genuine point. This does feel more like an arrival than a journey. Maybe that's just what spring does. Maybe part of spring's insistence is to seem like the whole point of there being seasons at all. Maybe it's not just semantics. Maybe in her playfulness Jennifer hit on some real wisdom. Maybe each good day is not actually part of a journey. Maybe each good day is itself a destination. An accomplishment. The place toward which you've been heading all along.

This morning is so ordinary. A little while ago we got Anya off to school in her blue uniform, red coat, and green backpack. She's recently had a haircut and now has bangs—"fringe" as they call it here. I had to lift the fine blond hair to plant a kiss on the warm skin of her forehead. Jennifer made avocado sandwiches for herself and Amy. I gave Amy a kiss and a squeeze, and they were out the door, Jennifer to the library and Amy to do some volunteer social work. I fixed myself a hot chocolate, climbed the stairs to my desk at the window, and turned on Classic FM. The famous "La donna é mobile" aria from *Rigoletto* filled the room (poor Rigoletto, never saw it coming). It's cloudy and the sea is calm. The tide is out, and the fishing boats are in, their hulls resting on the sheen of mud in the harbour. Ordinary. A gloriously ordinary day.

But what today might have been is an abyss at the back of my psyche.

Yesterday, on our way to Anya's horseback-riding lesson, we drove past a temporary sign propped on a tripod beside the rock-wall fence. In white letters on a blue metal background were the words "Serious accident here, April 23, Police appeal for witnesses."

A teenage girl from our village, we'd heard. An only child. We've been living here nine months, but we don't know her family. Most of the people we've met since moving to Scotland have primary-school-age children. Like us.

No doubt we've seen her, though. No doubt often. Up at the bakery or the fish and chips shop, or at the Christmas-tree-lighting party on the square, or walking with her friends along the stone seawall that encircles the tiny harbour out our cottage windows.

But we won't even know which of the young faces is missing. Wouldn't even know there was one fewer if we hadn't been told.

All I had to offer was the thought, *Poor someone—poor someone and her poor, poor parents* as we passed the sign and drove on through farm fields overlooking the North Sea. Anya's teacher Alice and the horses at Barnsmuir Farm were waiting.

"We're going to canter today," Anya said from the back seat. She could hardly contain herself.

When Anya had started her lessons last autumn, I'd been afraid. I always smiled and waved from behind the fence or from the parked car where Amy and I watched when she went by, and mostly I was able to push from my head the lines of Theodore Roethke's poem "Elegy for Jane: My Student, Thrown by a Horse." Every now and then, though, when I gave a thumbs-up or Amy took a picture of Anya sitting upright and trying not to smile beneath her helmet, a few of Roethke's words slipped in—"I remember the neckcurls . . . her quick look . . ."

Yes, I am a man who lives with, or, perhaps more accurately, who lives in spite of, a chronic awareness of potential disaster and the bottomless grief that is always threatening to open beneath every moment. Yes, my entire adult life, until I was thirty-six, I was periodically reminded by rapid and terrifying turns in my mother's precarious health that one's ordinary days could quite unceremoniously and brutally be taken away. A little fatigue could be the first sign of another heart attack. The onset of a mild fever might be the initial symptom of another life-threatening infection.

Time after time I was reminded: Grief waits. Everywhere. Always.

No one is safe. Ever. It's true.

And yet. And yet I choose to live without cowering. Well, usually without cowering. Sometimes the words of Roethke's poem whisper in my brain. "If only I could nudge you from this sleep, my maimed darling." Sometimes fear rules me. But not usually.

Anya fell once, earlier in the spring. It was a rainy day, so lessons were at an indoor arena near the farm. She was learning to jump, which was really just a little hop on the horse's part, over a bar maybe ten inches high. She'd been thrilled to have done it so well the previous lesson, and as she and the roan pony Blossom headed for the jump, her face was full of as much determination and confidence as I could remember seeing in any eight-year-old. But Blossom decided it wasn't enough determination and confidence and stopped suddenly just before the bar, sending Anya sliding off.

Amy gasped and held her hand to her mouth, but she stood her ground beside me. My wife is a tomboy, used to a little risk and rough and tumble. She didn't grow up with a mom in fragile health but in a family of downhill skiers and unflappable medical professionals who weren't about to flinch at every little bump and scrape. But it was everything I could do not to run to Anya, to stay standing in place, even though she was well clear of the horse's hooves and the fall hadn't looked too bad. The arena floor was four merciful inches deep with shredded rubber, and sure enough Anya was on her feet in a moment, climbing back on the horse with the help of one of Alice's teenage teaching assistants before I could have reached her had I dashed over. And instead of suffering the embarrassing scene I'd have made, she'd gotten a nice round of applause from the other girls and cleared the little jump on her next pass. Her first tumble had been a success for both Anya and me, and it was behind us. If anything, my fear watching the subsequent lessons eased a bit. It was possible for Anya to take a fall and be fine.

So even after passing that sign at the scene of the car wreck and sparing a thought for the poor someone I didn't know and her poor parents, I wasn't paying all that much mind to danger, to the unrelenting possibility for ruin. In fact, I was doing a bit of reveling in just how well everything was going for us since we'd moved here and in the beauty of this moment. Amy and I were sitting in the car, just beyond a few hundred blossoming daffodils at the edge of the sunny pasture, watching Anya and a couple other girls walking their ponies in a circuit while the blue sea rose beyond them. They stepped their horses over a couple of low jumps and wove them slowly between poles and curved around and repeated the route.

The wind lifted the horses' manes and tails and the girls' hair where it trailed from their helmets.

I looked down at the postcard I was writing to a friend. It was rather self-congratulatory, I admitted to myself, full of as much of our lucky life as I could fit.

"Good jump, Anya," Amy said with enthusiasm and encouragement, as if Anya could have actually heard her from a hundred yards across the windy field.

Apparently, the walk-through portion of the lesson was over. I put my postcard on the dash and looked up. My eyes scanned for Anya's red jacket and the white horse she was riding this time, Woody. A gray horse, I reminded myself. Alice had taught the girls that almost all white horses are properly called "grays."

Alice is about forty, around the same age as Amy and me. She is lean and beautiful and speaks with a refined English accent. She manages to seem poised in green, knee-high Wellington boots; a chore coat; and a bill cap. Like Amy, she is both gently kind and tough. Like my mom, too, it has occurred to me. But when Anya started lessons with her what mattered most about Alice to me was that we had asked around and heard she was the best riding instructor in our part of Scotland. And sure enough, she exuded the abilities and knowledge of someone who had known horses all her life.

"Well done, you!" I could faintly hear her call to Anya, whom I spotted on Woody just as he was coming down from another jump.

But there was a shriek, and then Woody was running faster.

A scream—Anya screaming.

Woody bolted, ran flat out, and Anya was screaming, "Mommy!" screaming, screaming, the horse down hard into its run, air whipping its mane back as it shot dangerously across the field with Anya on its back.

Nothing I could do.

Nothing.

Nothing.

The horse wasn't slowing but running thunderously, and Anya was screaming.

Amy and I ran from the car and sprinted toward the fence. The horse was running this way but in a curve so the fence wouldn't slow him.

"Mommy!" Anya screamed and bounced and jostled and clung on. She was in horrible danger. My child, my Anya.

"Whoa, whoa, WHOA!" I called as I ran, forcing my tone to be firm, not panicky.

But was the horse slowing? I couldn't tell. And I couldn't will the horse to slow. I couldn't will this to end OK. It just kept happening in front of me.

Amy and I reached the step-over at the fence and saw Anya fall off and the horse keep running away from where Anya hit the ground. We were over the fence and running toward her. *Please, oh please, oh please, let her stand up.*

And she stood up, wailing.

We reached her.

"Mommy," she cried in Amy's arms.

I scanned her, angled around to see her face, her eyes.

"I don't wanna do that again. I don't—I don't—I—I don't—" She was hysterical.

"It's OK, Baby, you're OK, you're all right, Anya," we said.

"Let me check you over, sweetheart," I said.

She limped slightly as she stepped back into a looser embrace with Amy. But what's a limp? I took her helmet off. I touched her head gently, her neck. I pressed my fingers on her abdomen, feeling for hard spots. I looked closely into her tear-welled eyes.

She was standing. She was crying and talking.

She hugged Amy again and sobbed.

Alice had reached us by now.

"I don't—I don't want to do that again!"

"Anya, Anya, no one's saying anything about that," Alice said with firm reassurance, though I could hear real fear under her words. "We just want to check you out." Alice looked her over. "You landed on your legs, yes?"

Anya nodded.

"You didn't hit your head?"

"No."

"Or your body, your torso?" I added.

"No."

Amy kept hold of her.

"Where did you hit?" I asked.

Anya pointed to her hip and the side of her thigh where flecks of grass were smeared onto her riding breeches.

"That's good," Alice said.

I wrapped Amy and Anya in my arms, and the smell of Anya's hair came to me with my breath. She was still here, still Anya. Unbroken.

A few steps and her limp was gone. A couple minutes more and Alice asked if she wanted to get back on Woody.

"*If* you want to," Alice said a second time.

What? *Back on?* I asked myself.

"Only if you want to," Amy and I both added.

The moment of truth was not just Anya's.

"Alice can lead you," I said as though it were just a suggestion, while in my racing mind it was an absolute requirement. The best thing to do after falling from a horse may be to get straight back on, but no way I was going to let that happen without Alice's firm grip on this horse's lead.

"That's right, Anya," Alice agreed. "I'll keep hold the whole time."

"It's your choice," Amy repeated. "We can be done for the day and come back next time, if you want."

"I want to stay." She wiped away her tears. "Can I ride some more? Is that OK?"

"Of course it is, Anya," Alice said. "Good girl."

"Of course you can, Baby," Amy repeated.

The best I could do was a nod and a weak "sure."

Alice's teenage assistant had fetched Woody from across the field. Alice clipped on the lead. Then Anya followed Alice's example and stroked the horse's nose and neck. Then Anya's shin was in Alice's cupped hands, and Alice was hoisting my child, my sweet child, the most direct evidence I know of divinity, back onto that horse.

As promised, Alice walked them back to the poles and jumps and never let go of the lead as she, Woody, and Anya walked around the circuit. Subdued by what they'd seen, the other girls also spent these last few minutes of the lesson walking their horses.

Amy and I stood in the field, unwilling to retreat back to the car. We passed a few quiet comments back and forth. She would have been just as happy to go home and never let Anya near a horse again, but she thought it was good that Anya wanted to get back on. I agreed with both positions.

"That was so horrible," I added.

Amy's expression collapsed, and she held her hand to her mouth. Tears rolled down her cheeks.

"I was so helpless. She was screaming for me."

I put my arm around her. "She's OK," I said. "But God, that *was* horrible."

Amy nodded. She took a side step away from me. She was determined to keep herself together for Anya's sake, for the moment.

I felt the soft, rockless grass under my feet, looked over at two big, jagged logs not twenty yards away.

At the end of the lesson, Alice gathered her horseback pupils around. Amy and I could hear her explain how what had happened hadn't been Anya's fault, how these things just happen sometimes.

"But I want all of you to remember, you must never, never scream. All right? If you scream it frightens the pony and makes it run faster. That's very important."

Back at the stables, as Alice hung up saddles and blankets and her teenage assistant and the girls, including Anya, led the horses to turn them out into the pasture, Alice explained to Amy and me that she warns her students about screaming. She doesn't do it at the very first; she doesn't want to scare them, she said. But early on, when they're still just walking the horses, the first time someone gives a little shout of any kind, she tells them about screaming and how dangerous it can be.

"I'm terribly sorry. I don't think that ever happened with Anya. She's so calm. I didn't think to warn her because she never shouts."

We nodded.

"She was doing so well today, too."

"I know," Amy said. I noticed her voice was steady again, for the time being anyway.

"This wind can make a horse jumpy, too," Alice went on. "But even so, if Woody ever does anything like that again, just once, he's off the farm."

I asked if Anya could ride a totally bombproof horse for the next few lessons—to which Alice readily agreed—and if there was anything else we could do to keep it from happening again.

Alice said you can never be sure it won't happen and added that sometimes Anya was a bit eager to run before she'd learned to walk, that from the first day she'd been asking when she'd get to jump.

I couldn't help but smile. My little embracer of life.

"So it's a balance with her," Alice continued, "between encouraging that confidence and holding her back until she's ready."

Yes, that's exactly it, I thought to myself, one of the great cruxes of parenting for me.

Alice said she'd give Anya a couple special lessons, one a non-riding lesson in which she'll handle a horse, really assert herself with the animal and get her hands on it, its hooves and head and body, and another lesson in which she'll practice nothing but stops.

Anya walked back toward us.

"Well done, you," Alice said. "Getting back on Woody like that."

Anya gave a weak smile.

"All right then?"

Anya nodded and gave a grin that was a bit forced, but a grin nonetheless.

"I want to keep riding."

At home later, when I went up to Anya's room to check on her, she was lying on the floor, drawing a girl on horseback in magic marker. I asked how she felt.

"Anything sore?"

"No, Daddy," she said with exasperation.

"Look at me a sec."

Her eyes were bright.

I felt her abdomen. No hard or tender spots.

"I'm *fine*."

"Sorry, Bug, I'm going to keep checking every fifteen or twenty minutes."

"Thirty," she insisted. Her friend Callum Stamper from up the road was due for a play date soon. I knew she didn't want any more of my nonsense in front of him than necessary.

"All right, thirty," I said. I didn't say I'd just trade off checking every fifteen minutes or so with her mother.

After Callie came over and was upstairs playing with Anya, Amy and I stood in the kitchen chopping smoked fish and onions for soup.

"I think that was the scariest thing that's happened since she was born," Amy said.

"I think you're right."

"I just keep seeing it." Amy's face contorted in pain again, and tears streamed down her cheeks. She said she wanted to talk to someone about this, someone who knew something about horses. Our lack of experience was a problem. She needed someone with some perspective.

"Right away," she said. "Who do we know?"

I got my aunt Charleen in Louisiana on the phone. Charleen has ridden since she was a little girl. More importantly for me, though, this was as close as I could come to calling my mom. Unlike me, my mom didn't fret over danger, even the ever-present danger of her own fragile health. "We have today," she'd say. "And we don't get today back." And unlike me, my mother had a clear sense of the difference between worrying over someone and nurturing them.

Charleen's advice aligned pretty much with Alice's plan to help Anya rebuild her confidence by having her handle the horse and practice her stops. I thanked her and handed the phone to Amy.

My mom and her sister were separated when their parents' deaths left them orphans, my mom at seventeen and Charleen at twelve. Charleen was sent to live with relatives in Louisiana. My mother stayed in Los Angeles with a foster family until she could finish high school and move in with their older brother. My mother and her sister spent precious little time together after that, but they remained deeply connected. In adulthood Charleen's horses kept her close to home, and my parents were usually too broke to travel as they pursued various degrees and teaching posts that kept my family moving from university to university for years. But the sisters talked on the phone, sometimes all afternoon. As Amy listened to Charleen, I remembered my mom at our own kitchen table when I was a kid, her feet propped up on a chair, a pink can of Tab in one hand and the receiver in the other, laughing with abandon, speaking in soft conspiratorial tones, sometimes consoling, sometimes—like Amy now—being consoled.

And whatever Charleen said to Amy apparently managed to console her some. She made it to Anya's bedtime without coming unglued, and I did the same.

Anya got her bath, pulled on her pj's, and brushed her teeth as she'd done a thousand nights before. She was under the covers, and Amy and I were climbing into bed with her for our nightly Harry Potter reading when Anya's magic-marker girl on horseback caught my eye. I reached over to her little desk and picked up the drawing.

"Tell me about this," I said.

"It's me on Woody."

"You're smiling."

"Yeah."

"How are you doing?"

"I'm *fine*, I keep telling you," she said with a huff.

"I'm proud of you for getting back on," Amy said. "I talked to Aunt Charleen today, and do you know what she told me?"

"What?"

"She told me she fell off a runaway horse when she was ten."

"She did?"

"And Sheila was there. Your Nana. And she told Charleen to get back on and Charleen did. And she kept on riding horses the rest of her childhood after that. And into her adulthood. It's given her many years of great joy."

"I bet Nana encouraged her more than told her," I added.

I couldn't imagine my mom, even as a fourteen- or fifteen-year-old, *telling* a ten-year-old to do anything so frightening. She must have *encouraged*. Must have helped her sister up and held her and then dusted her off and asked if she might want to give it another try.

Ah, how limited is the child in his ability to see his parents as they might have been long before they were his parents. Clearly, Charleen had meant the story as an account of her sister's wisdom, as a link between what Anya's Nana had said and what Anya had done almost fifty years later. But I wanted more. I wanted what's forever beyond me now. I wanted my mother's tone and the exact words she'd have chosen this time, for Amy and me, and for Anya. The reassurance and guidance I wanted was from my mother, not the teenage Sheila MacLure as I could only imagine her. But now they were both gone.

What was left, though, what remained, was what she taught. The wonder and value of every day. And every night. I cracked the thick Harry Potter book to keep Anya on schedule, to give her the comfort of an ordinary night.

As it happened, we found Harry, Ron, and Hermione on a dragon, clinging to the panicked beast as it soared out of their control, out of London, all the way to Scotland.

"Like you on Woody," I said before thinking better of it.

"Daddy!" she snapped, reproach and a little woundedness in her voice.

"I'm sorry," I said. "That wasn't kind." Anya knew the seriousness of what had happened to her, the terror of that sprinting horse, its whipping mane, her so small and in such peril on its back, jostling and bouncing helplessly, clinging on and then falling anyway. She hadn't let it get the better of her. She'd chosen courage. But what had happened to her was not to be relegated to the realm of joke or fantasy and play.

We got Harry, Ron, and Hermione safely down off their dragon and closed the book for the night despite Anya's protestations.

"Just a little more?"

"Sorry, Sweetie. School tomorrow," I said, and Amy and I tucked her in.

"Nana nest," I said, fluffing her comforter and pillow around her head like my mom used to do for me. I kissed my girl's forehead and lingered, feeling her warmth against my lips, her living warmth.

"Mommy?" Anya called when we'd turned out the light and made our way out the door. "Will you lie with me?"

"Of course, Baby."

I looked back through the doorway and watched my wife snuggling in next to our child.

An ordinary sight.

How can I thank God? How do I speak to the spirit of creation, the power of existence over nonexistence, to the Love in All Things, and say thank you for my child's life, that it goes on and she is unbroken? How do I say this when there are parents in this world for whom today was the first in a lifetime of days in which Ordinary is the name of a lost paradise?

I don't know how I can say it.

I don't know how I can't.

I look out the window over my desk, out over the enormity and indifference of the sea, into I know not what. I think of that warm skin on Anya's forehead against my lips last night, and again this morning, and in a voice beyond fear and courage, in a voice simply grateful, I say it.

"Thank you."

MARQUETTE, DAY FIVE

FEBRUARY 6 . . .

This morning my sister washed our mother's hair in the bathroom sink. Mother and daughter, touching.

A couple times Mom asked to see Amy, which made Amy happy when she arrived from her parents' house with Anya.

Mom has managed to stay out of bed and in her wheelchair, but she has been pretty deep in a stupor, mostly. Now and then, though, she works her way back up enough to smile and say occasional words.

Anya did her little ballet dance turns for her, and Mom opened her eyes and actually focused on Anya. Anya told her about the kids magazine My Big Backyard *and talked to her about what was in it. Mom lifted her head and smiled when Anya mentioned a chipmunk. Anya explained the magazine comes every month, just for her.*

"Your own special . . . ," Mom managed to say before drifting off.

A short time later we were sitting around her, talking, and Amy said, "Anya's been saying she wants to see Nana Banana." Amy reminded us all that Nana calls Anya, "Anya Lasagna."

We tried to think of a rhyme for Daddy.

"Laddy? Maddy?"

We all sat for a while, then I said, "Daddy how fatty," and Mom actually laughed*! Smiled and laughed! Suddenly, with the rest of us.*

Later, I read "I Wandered Lonely as a Cloud" to her again.

I told her again I was there with her.

Earlier, at one point when Anya was dancing and Mom had her eyes open to watch, she looked from Anya to me, right into my eyes. She leaned slightly my way and tilted her head against mine.

There was a moment today when Charleen was talking to her about being her Cheerio-eating buddy and Mom looked at her and managed a smirk.

When my old college friend Rick came out from talking to her, he said she called him a dirty rat for driving all the way up here from his home downstate.

Somehow she's enjoying all the company.

Amazing.

Why should she have to leave now, with such a life she's built?

I slept and dreamed Death was a cat-sized tan cricket, waiting to chew her wounds.

Amy said she took Anya to the local-artisan-made-goods store, Michigan Fair, and there was a fountain, and with every penny Anya threw in she said, "I wish Nana would get better. I wish Nana could walk again."

Scotland, May

Anya cups her hands at her temples to shade the window's glass from the lamp on her desk behind her. Many months ago, she learned by heart how long to wait between flashes so she'll be answered when she says "goodnight" to the lighthouse on the Isle of May. Two flashes, fourteen seconds, two flashes. Like two syllables of reply.

Once, before GPS and radar, sailors nearing shore from the darkness or a storm could know their location by the unique flash signature of each lighthouse. Maybe before it dies, a good language matures to speak something of love. Certainly our lighthouse is doing what it—"she" to Anya—has always done, offering steady reassurance to the traveler. Saying, "You're here."

In Venice the rain held off just long enough. We rode a low, wide boat from the airport and stepped off at the quay alongside the Grand Canal. Amy's old friend Nikki, her husband, Edmundo, and their three-year-old daughter, Cecelia, strolled with Amy, Anya, and me beside docks crowded with gondolas and past kiosks with maps, handbags, postcards, and gondola key chains for sale.

I asked Anya if this wasn't one of the most beautiful cities she'd ever seen.

"Not really," she said without a trace of malice in her voice. As if giving her considered opinion. "I mean, it looks like any other city."

"Hmm . . . ," I replied. "Some people say it's the most beautiful city in the world."

"Who says that?" she asked, as if honestly curious.

"Oh, lots of people," I said, though I'm sure she realized that nobody specific had come to mind. She had her rhapsodic father over a barrel. All she had to do was play it cool. I was to remember that she'd come willingly but not enthusiastically.

Just four days before, when I'd first mentioned the idea of this trip to her, she'd asked if it was all right if she said she didn't want to go.

I was surprised, but I shouldn't have been. We've really had her on the run, more than ever before in her whole life, all this gallivanting in addition to having uprooted her to move to another country in the first place.

"I'd be disappointed," I had answered her. "But of course I want to know how you feel or I wouldn't have asked."

I'd asked why she wasn't excited to go, and, no surprise, she'd said she'd had enough of other places for a while and just wanted to be at home.

"I mean, our Crail home," she'd added quickly.

I'd gone on to explain that the trip would be a kind of double birthday present for her mom. She'd get to go to Venice, to revisit another place, like Paris, that she and I had gone when we were young and first in love. And she'd get to see Nikki, one of her oldest and dearest friends, whom Amy had met when Nikki was a high school exchange student in the US and who lives not far from Venice.

"Can I think about it?" Anya had asked.

I confess, I'd been frustrated. I was asking the kid if she wanted to go to *Venice*. I'd reminded myself she was eight.

"OK, give it a think. But we will need to decide today, if we're going to try to get there by her birthday, and if Nikki's going to get time off work to join us."

"All right, Daddy."

And sure enough, later that afternoon, after asking her mom about her Italian friend Nikki, and if she was sad that she wouldn't be seeing her while they were on the same side of the ocean, Anya had opened the door to our bedroom to find me writing at my desk and told me she wanted to do this. "For Mama."

Over dinner we'd told Amy she had an early present. Anya had handed her a homemade card with a drawing of Amy in a gondola on the front and construction paper tickets inside.

Now, as we strolled from the boat toward Piazza San Marco, Anya was momentarily a little impressed in spite of herself by the sight of the famed winged Lion of Venice sculpture atop its pillar.

"A hundred points, Daddy!" she exclaimed, beginning the game of "find the most lions" we'd planned.

And in spite of herself a little wonder may have crept in when we turned the corner onto the Piazzetta San Marco. The view opened to the bell tower, the Basilica, and the enormous main plaza itself as a thousand statues rose with the arches and columns in the architecture around us. Best of all, there were the pigeons, descendants of the ones we'd told her about, the ones for whom Amy had sat as a human perch and fed from her open hands twenty-one years ago. They rose in flight in front of Cecelia toddling along as Anya took her hand, and we made our way across the piazza toward the labyrinth of streets and our hotel.

We all checked in, and Amy, Anya, and I stepped into our room one flight above a quiet narrow lane off the Calle Frezzeria. I pulled back the curtains, opened the tall windows, and pushed out the shutters. Across the narrow canyon of a back street was a sun-bleached stucco building with shuttered windows of its own and an awning below.

After we'd all unpacked, we wandered, looking at restaurant menu boards and sidewalk tables until we found Al Buso next to the Rialto Bridge, with a table for six right against the marble railing beside the canal.

The thing about seeing someone you've known since they were seventeen is they still seem seventeen. Nikki's daughter, Cecelia, seemed exactly what she is, a little girl of nearly four. Nikki's husband, Edmundo, quiet and dark and lean, seemed his age, about fifty. And to anyone passing by, I'm sure Nikki looked forty, as did Amy and I. But to me, Nikki was Nikki in high school, just as Amy and I were the people we were then, only somehow married and with a daughter of nearly nine. Feeling the same person you were when you were young is generally less lamentable (if not less suspect) when an old friend across the table is so clearly the person she was.

Amy and Nikki laughed about the old days and friends, which made those days and friends also seem less former and lost. We sat for hours while the narrow swath of sky above the narrow stretch of the Grand Canal got dark and the lamps began to reflect amber and white in the crossing, blending wakes of water taxis and cargo boats and gondolas. The spaghetti frutti di mare was fine, but the espresso afterward was the best I can remember. Maybe it was the deep, sweet scent of Nikki and Edmundo's cigarettes.

Later, back at the hotel after hours at our restaurant table and hours more wandering, Anya said she likes Venice. I opened the tall windows again and pushed open the shutters just in time for us to hear the rain begin on the awning below, and the three of us snuggled in to read our next installment of Harry Potter.

Now Amy and Anya are fast asleep in the big double bed. A church bell somewhere bonged midnight not long ago. I'm sitting shirtless on the daybed beside the open window, writing by the dim light of a streetlamp mounted high on the wall outside, listening to the splattering of rain on the wet stone pavement below and the taps of the drops on the awning canvas. Tonight, I write as a thank-you to my mother for this glorious life, this moment of solitude, my sleeping loves, the lightest of breezes entering with the sound of Venice rain.

We walked slowly, with our hands behind our backs, Edmundo and I. We had no language to share and nothing I knew of in common, except the love of our wives, who walked a few steps ahead of us, and of our daughters, a few steps ahead of them, and so we strolled beside the Grand Canal in silence. This morning, over breakfast on the rooftop terrace of our hotel where a jumble of tile roofs and tiled chimneys and rooftop gardens spread around us to the near horizon of bell towers and steeples and spires, Nikki told me that Edmundo says I walk fast, so all the rest of the day I eased into his pace, this man watching his wife laugh like a teenager beside mine as they talked about teenage things—dances and boys and nights running from police cars.

Under the watchful stone gaze of the Giardini Pubblici statuary, Edmundo and I stopped and stood in silence to watch my daughter take his daughter's hand and lead her from playground swings to seesaw to slide. At a café table along Via Giuseppe Garibaldi we sat and watched our girls in the shade across the lane as they made a game of Cecelia trotting off and Anya guiding her back toward us. And we watched the girls' moms talk and laugh some more.

When they'd asked all they could think to ask about each other's families, Nikki turned to me and asked how long it had been since my mom died.

I was caught off guard to be drawn in. I'd been enjoying watching their grand conversation, comfortable as the audience, with another delicious espresso.

"My mom—" I had to think. About a month seemed the answer. "Five years."

"She was very good, your mom."

"Yes."

"I remember. I am sorry."

"Thank you. It's a different planet without her," I said. And suddenly I no longer felt the same person I used to be in those days when Amy and I first knew Nikki. I felt very far from that person.

"No matter how old you are, you are never ready. When my grandmother dies—died—my mother says she is a tree without its root."

"Yes. A boat forever cut loose from shore."

Nikki lifted her sunglasses onto her forehead to reveal her eyes. I remembered how a conversation with her could turn that fast, that easily, to the deep, real flesh under the skin.

"My mother says nobody will ever call her 'my bambina' again."

I took my own sunglasses off and agreed, "If your mother loves you well, you are never loved like that again."

"You miss her, too," Nikki said to Amy.

"Yes. We were very good friends. She was the kindest person I've ever known."

Nikki paused to translate for Edmundo. He nodded empathetically as she caught him up. The thought that Amy, Anya, and I could have moved to Italy instead of Scotland drifted into my mind. We could have sat in the shade of awnings for hours like this with Nikki and Edmundo, watching our girls and talking about family in a country renowned for talking about family.

As things were, though, we saw Nikki, Edmundo, and little Cecelia off in the shade of a newspaper kiosk beside the dock near

San Marco. Anya squeezed Cecelia and called her Chi Chi like her parents did and lifted her off her feet. Edmundo embraced me. He kissed my cheek and looked me in the eye and clapped me on the shoulder. Nikki hugged and kissed us all and came back from the dock for more hugs and kisses.

"You are so great, Amos," she sobbed Amy's nickname from many years ago. "I am so happy we were together."

Amy wiped her eyes.

She has made a life out of Anya and me. She's got her work, work about which she's passionate, but all through her thirties that work has taken a place behind her family. She's got friends, but they are *our* friends, friends we've made together.

Nikki, though, was Amy's first, ours second. And with Nikki Amy seemed to find a certain old happiness she doesn't get often enough anymore.

I know she doesn't regret a moment she's given to Anya or me. I know we are her life's greatest joy and meaning. But as I watched her watching her old friend's boat pull away, I also knew there were other meanings and joys for which Amy was overdue.

Today is Mother's Day in the US. Mother's Day somewhere else. That fits. Today I give bitterness its due. Here is the Scottish coast, the still surface of the North Sea in the sunshine. Here are the fishing boats just offshore. And today is a Mother's Day my mother doesn't get.

For all the superhuman optimism and kindness and gratitude with which my mother lived her life, that life was taken from her. Slowly. Painfully. Inch by gangrened, infected, throbbing inch. As she watched. How many times I remember she held up her hand to show me how far the darkness had moved down a finger or where a finger had been taken to another knuckle. This after nothingness rose like a tide to take her feet. And on the merry world rolls without her.

For British Mothering Sunday, up on the shore of Loch Shiel back in March, I had heart. I felt an optimism and gratitude befitting my mother's son. Today I come up short of my mother's grace. Today I have only loyalty to her. Let me be an exile from a day that does not have her.

For the sake of Amy, to whom such holidays matter and whom I love through every bitterness and who is a wonderful mom, I'll join Anya in marking the day with flowers, a card, dinner out in St. Andrews. For those I love, I will do as my mother must have done countless times for me and muster a geniality from the gloom. But in the solitary world of my heart I permit myself the weakness to begrudge the world for the nothing it has today to give her.

Four thousand two hundred and twenty-four pages. The Harry Potter series, start to finish.

Last night Anya, Amy, and I sat cross-legged on Anya's bed. Usually, we're snuggled in when we read, but not last night. Last night was the end, the arrival. No way Anya was going to just lie down. In fact, when we came upstairs to read, she did a summersault on her bed.

Better yet, she wanted to take turns reading. We made our way toward the end, each of us reading a page then passing the giant, open volume along. Anya needed a little help with *emphasized*, but she got *inherited*, *evidently*, and *ecstatically* with only the slightest hesitation.

This is the last month of her eighth year. We've been reading the books to her, off and on, since she was five. More than a third of her life. Way more than half of the life she remembers.

"What's Little Lamb think of us getting to the end of the books?" I asked. She had her constant companion tucked under her arm. Things were getting tense. Which beloved characters would live and which would die?

"She's fine. She says the books are a side thing to our plays."

"She's right," Amy offered. "And I think J. K. Rowling would very much approve of that."

Amy added that, just like other characters who'd died in earlier books, anyone who didn't survive in this last installment would go right on living in our games.

"I know," Anya said. "But let's read now, OK?"

And so on we pressed and learned, with a few tears, who does and who does not survive, and then we came to the epilogue, a little glimpse into how life goes on in the future. Into every third sentence or so, Rowling had planted reasons for delight and satisfaction, for the belief in a world that remakes itself from its past.

Rowling lost her own mother when she was just starting the first book. She has spoken about how that loss goes on. She's said she regrets that her mother never knew Harry. I regret that mine didn't either. She'd have found a lot to like in the fellow orphan who builds a new life based on love. And she'd have played right along with Amy, Anya, and me. She would have made an excellent Professor McGonagall.

But like Amy and me, Rowling also has children of her own, new souls for whom this new world is the only world there is. The comfort of life's perpetual renewal, the only lasting comfort there is, really, is the truth she wrote into her epic's final scene. The world's new children are the next protagonists, the great and ongoing story's next heroes.

As it happened, the very last page of the book arrived on Anya's turn to read. While she read it, I thought about all the places we've tucked her into bed and read from Harry's story—her bedroom back in Washington state, the gable bedroom atop Amy's parents' log house in upper Michigan, the bedroom in which my mother died in Marquette. We finished the third book in the loft of our tiny Idaho cabin by head lamp because the cabin doesn't have electricity. On all fours as a stag, Anya had jumped back and forth between the loft beds while I'd read, and we'd learned which characters had all along been able to change into animals. We've read it in hotel rooms in London, Paris, Dublin, and Venice, in an Irish farmhouse, in motels in Montana. We've stood beside the loch where filmmakers set Hogwarts Castle and on the knoll on which they built Hagrid's hut. We've found the luggage trolley disappearing into Platform Nine and Three-Quarters in King's Cross Station; been to Edinburgh's Elephant House tearoom, where much of the first two books got written; and ran around on broomsticks in our American backyard. Back in the Washington bedroom where we started our reading four years ago, I've painted the walls with mountains towering over a quidditch pitch, Hagrid's hut, and the loch-side castle. The castle windows I painted with glow-in-the-dark paint, and I did the same for the sun above. When we turn out Anya's light, the sun becomes the shining moon and the windows of Hogwarts glow invitingly.

The books have given us an imaginative life we can share, a sense of wonder about the world. We've walked through shopping malls playing "wizard or muggle?" as we pass other shoppers (hint, teenage kids with dyed hair and dressed in lots of black are always witches or wizards). Driving Anya to school, I've pushed and pushed the red defrost button on the dash while Amy rolled her eyes and said, "Ronald, haven't you gotten that invisibility booster fixed yet?" While we've driven Anya up to her Highland-dance class in St. Andrews, she's howled from the back seat, paused, and said, "It's Professor McGonagall as a cat, and she does *not* like riding in cars!"

I'm loyal to the former world in which my mother lived, but I also love this life of ours, this new world in which we live, into which my mother wished me, as all parents wish their children. I only wish I could show her more of this new story, this story in which Anya is the hero, than the little epilogue we got.

Last night, in our snug Scottish cottage where we finished the last of the last book, when Anya was finally under the Harry Potter quilt Amy's mother had made for her, and we'd kissed her forehead, and Amy'd told her sweet dreams and gone downstairs, and when I'd clicked off the lamp, I stood in her doorway and said, "G'night, Harry."

"G'night, Ron," she returned with a satisfied, drowsy sigh.

All through May, the harbour has grown steadily busier with sightseers. Yesterday was bright and warm, and there were even more than usual, photographing boats, one another on the seawall, the Isle of May on the horizon, our cottage. Whenever I looked up from my writing desk I wondered if any of them were the next renters, a couple from Denmark here to see their new home.

What would they look like? The harbour was crawling with couples. They have two young boys, but they'd left them behind for their reconnaissance trip.

And then there they were, no doubt about it. Tall and lanky, about the same age as Amy and me. They stood at the bottom of the stairs to our front garden and took in the cottage. He had long hair and a beard. She had short blond hair. They both had looks of wonderment at their good fortune. He raised his hand, and she paid him a high five.

If a three-hundred-and-seventy-some-year-old cottage teaches you anything, it teaches you that, sooner or later, we are all replaced.

I opened the window and leaned out.

"I bet I know who you are," I called down.

The delight on Morten's and Maria's faces never faded as we showed them around. The narrow stone fireplace in the snug little living room, the tiny kitchen with its tiny fridge and big wooden table for six, the bathtub with the view to the harbour and sea, the same view out Anya's bedroom window above the little window seat on which she's sat so many nights to tell the Isle of May Lighthouse goodnight, my desk at our bedroom window, the tiny guest cottage out back, the terraced back garden with its view out over the cottage chimneys to fishing boats working the lobster pots out past the seawall. In two months it would all be theirs.

Amy and I sat at the kitchen table over tea with them and told them the fishermen are reticent (or, OK, curmudgeonly) but when they see you walking out the door with your child in a Crail School uniform they'll know you're not just on holiday and they'll start to nod or even say hello. We told them the best place to get acquainted with people in the village is the school gate. Carl the mechanic is fair and good, I said, though between his accent and yours you won't understand much of what each other says.

They laughed. They were enchanted. A new life. Like me, Morten's a professor with a year sabbatical to devote to his own work. Like Amy, Maria's a mom excited but a little anxious about how she'll make friends and fill her time. They both wonder how their kids will get on.

The world replaces us all.

My mom trusted and welcomed that about the world. It was something she loved about academic life, the cars with their hazards flashing and trunks open on the sidewalks beside the dorms every autumn and again every spring. Human beings taking places left them by human beings who depart. She had faith in how the world was made. If the human seasons saddened or frightened her, she rarely if ever said so. Instead, she spoke often of the comfort she found in the cycles that create and take us.

Amy wants to go home more than I do. Like Anya, she's ready for our house, our old friends, the feel of American coins in her hand, the right-hand side of wide roads. So I was surprised when she told me how hard it was for her to think of being replaced here.

"This is our little cottage. Our village."

"But you want to go home."

"I know. It still bothers me to think of someone else here, though. I can't help it."

"I get that," I said as we lay in bed, our curtains open to the lighthouse blinking, the inky sea, and a sky that grows more stubborn in its refusal to go dark every night. "It makes me happy to think of them here, though. Did you hear Morten? He says 'man.'"

In his Dutch accent he'd addressed me with the term: "This place is unbelievable, man." As anyone who knows me can tell you, "man" is one of my favorite terms of address. Morten and Maria will bathe their kids in this tub, they'll make love in this bed and wake to the waves out this window. They'll argue in the kitchen over the same tiny steel sink. They'll meet friends in the village, and when one of those friends comes over for dinner, Morten will address him as "man."

Meanwhile the sun comes out for at least a while every day. Meanwhile we have a little less than two months in which to live the last of our lives here. In which to let the end that is coming teach us each day that remains.

There's a photo we keep on our fridge back in Washington of Cousin Jennifer as a smiling towhead of about three on a pony. When Anya first noticed the picture she was just a little older than Jennifer was at the time it was taken, and she asked when she'd been on that horse. They look that much like older and younger versions of each other.

There's enough difference in their ages that they never squabble; Jennifer's an adult and became so about the time she moved in with us as a college freshman. Anya can look up to her in the uncomplicated way in which a child can admire someone completely beyond her own stage of development. But Jennifer's also the most playful, guileless adult I know. She's completely at home spending hours playing Harry Potter or making forts on the rocky shore or holding a rope as a musher behind Anya as a sled dog tugging her around the house. Having Jennifer with us here has taken a little of the homesickness from Anya's spring. To Anya, Jennifer shines as a sister.

Now though, Jennifer was headed off for a six-week backpacking tour around Europe, and Anya was distraught. After we said good-bye at the train station near St. Andrews, she bawled inconsolably.

"I miss her!" she sobbed from the back seat as I drove the twisty road toward Crail through the seemingly eternal dusk.

"I do too, Sweetie," Amy agreed.

"Me too," I said. "But we'll all be together again in the fall."

"But just for one more year. Then she'll be gone and never live with us again."

Anya is coming to that age at which, more and more, she feels the weight of even distant eventualities.

"Maybe you'll move in with her when you're in college," I offered. But right away I knew I'd said the wrong thing.

"I don't want to leave you!" she cried.

"No, no. You wouldn't have to."

"Daddy just means she'll go on being a part of our family. You two will have each other all your lives."

And it was true. God willing, Anya and Jennifer will live a long time. And after Amy and I and the other people older than them in our families have gone, Anya and Jennifer will have each other to remember by and to know in that thorough, lifelong way of siblings.

"I don't want her to *go*!" Anya wept on and wasn't to be consoled.

It's horrible to hear your child cry. The urge to make it better, right away, is biological and overwhelming. It was all I could do to focus on the road curving through woods and along stone walls through the long dusk. It's particularly torturous when your child cries for an inescapable sorrow she's just apprehended is woven into the very fabric of existence. The sorrow that sooner or later we lose one another.

But as hard as it was to hear Anya grieve, I also rejoiced a little inside. She was grieving because she loves.

The three of us were cozy in the cottage living room. Amy'd been dealing the cards for an evening game of There's a Moose in the House. Anya and I had cooling mugs of hot chocolate. Then the phone rang in the kitchen. It was an old friend calling from America to see how I'm holding up as word of the movie *Bright Star* starts to get out.

Fine tonight until this call was the truth. I'd wanted nothing more than to hang up midsentence, as if we'd been cut off, and go back to the living room and pretend the phone had never rung. But a friend who has known you half your life and still believes in you even, or especially, when you're knocked down is rare and precious, so I called out to Amy and Anya I'd be a minute and sat down at the kitchen table and proceeded to tell my friend that sometimes it was every bit as bad as she might guess.

After I'd hung up and was back at the card game, Anya asked me what was as bad as my friend might guess.

Just a writing thing, I explained and promised to tell her about it later. I laid down a moose card in her mother's house and did my best to gloat convincingly.

Later came, and as I put away our clean cocoa mugs and wiped down the kitchen counter, to my surprise Anya remembered to ask me about my complaint.

"Well," I sighed. "Remember all those pages taped to my office walls back home? I was writing a movie, one I'd been planning to write ever since I became an adult. It was about a true story, one nobody had ever made into a movie before. And then a few months ago I was finally almost done when I found out that somebody else had just made a movie of the same story. Their version of the same story."

I read her face as she took it all in, listening and considering intently.

"I've been really, really sad about it. Really sad. But I'm still happy deep down, because I have you and Mama and we have these wonderful days in Scotland."

Her lips pursed and her eyes reddened.

"Daddy." Tears rolled down her cheeks. She sobbed and hugged me. "I grew up with you writing that movie!"

"Oh, Baby, I'm all right. I'm disappointed but I'll be OK."

"Why did someone else get to write it? It's not fair."

You said it, kid. Goddamn, brutally unfair.

That voice was there in my head, but Anya's thin arms squeezed me tighter, and I heard another voice.

A good life.

What your parents do about their own suffering can reveal depths in them beyond who they manage to be for you when they are safe and comfortable. I loved my mother as a woman of great patience and kindness. Then they began to cut pieces of her off, and I met a soul of exquisite grace and wisdom.

And the amputation of my screenplay dream, of any dream, no matter how deep its sinews go, is hardly the amputation of a foot. We grow new dreams.

"I'm jealous of the person who got to have her movie made," I confessed. "But you know what else? I admire her too. She must be someone I'd like a lot if she also wanted to tell that story. And even though nobody will want to make another movie about it right now, I made mine into a play. And now I'm writing it as a book, a novel." I added a conspiratorial "shhh." Countless times she's heard me say I don't talk about what I'm working on.

Amy ducked in through the doorway. She'd been listening.

"I feel the same way as you, Anya. It just crushes me. But I'm so glad you're empathetic with Daddy and what disappoints him."

"It isn't fair."

"No, it isn't."

"It's just really bad luck," I offered.

With another squeeze Anya released me, and for something to do with myself I went back to wiping the counters while we talked.

"What's the story?"

"It's about John Keats, one of my two favorite poets, and how he fell in love with the girl next door, whose name was Fanny Brawne. But then he got very sick and died."

"Why do you want to write about something sad?"

"Mmm . . . good question." In fact, she'd gone right to the heart of things.

"How come?"

"Well, we learn things about people when they're sad. And it's not all sad, not deep down."

I sat down and hoisted her onto my knee. "Keats got sick and died, but he learned to love. Everyone dies, but not everyone learns to love. It's very hard for some people."

"Why?"

She wanted to know, but I also recognized she had—and wanted to keep—such thorough attention from me, wanted to engage me on this level, close to my adult heart.

"Well, sometimes they're afraid of losing people. Keats's daddy died when he was a boy. And then his mom."

An orphan like my mother. I've devoted the best of my imagination to him for years because of the beauty in his poetry, but also in an attempt to understand how a soul grows from such loss and grief to become so enormous and embracing.

"And his brother died, too," Amy added. If nobody else ever comes to know my Keats and Fanny, Amy knows them from reading draft after draft.

"I've got to keep living with Keats and Fanny," I explained to Anya. "So I keep writing, no matter what. Until I know them as well as I can."

"Like J. K. Rowling with Harry, Ron, and Hermione," she said.

"Yeah, like J. K. Rowling with Harry, Ron, and Hermione."

She gave me another squeeze.

"I'm sorry, Daddy."

"Thank you, Bug."

It was past her bedtime, but I told her if she'd get her pj's on and teeth brushed right away, I'd tell a story. I was beaten and sad, and Anya was powerless to stop that. But the parent she saw, the parent I found in myself, refused to be bitter or defeated.

Then, when I turned out the kitchen light and stood and listened to the creaks of her and Amy climbing the stairs, it occurred to me that maybe Anya wasn't powerless in the face of my suffering after all. Maybe she was essential to my transcendence. Maybe I'd been essential to my mother's.

Marquette, Day Six

February 7, morning . . .

It's been snowing since Amy, Anya, and I arrived in Marquette, and it continues to snow. Why should Mom have to die in the grip of winter, she who so loves the sun and flowers? She cannot go outside, has not been able to all week.

I was up a great deal of the night, Ann and Dad and me with Mom, Dad beside her, Ann lying on the floor, me in a chair, all of us saying over and over, "It's OK, we're here, we love you," like a mantra as she breathed hard and seemed so scared beneath her furrowed brow.

Then she'd settle for a while.

Once she said, "Your voices. Good."

Finally, we all slept a few hours.

I'd thought that we were at the end, but here it is, late morning, and her life goes on.

I will write her obituary today. By her side.

Scotland, Late Spring and Early Summer

Anya is nine. Amy and I brought her and three of her school friends down to Edinburgh on the train for a birthday celebration of Anya's design—the playground in Princess Street Gardens beneath the city's hilltop castle, a stuffed animal store, Starbucks for hot chocolate. As the girls laughed and held hands and ran ahead on park paths and city sidewalks, I watched to learn what nine might mean for my daughter.

What I saw was empathy. One of the girls was lagging behind, maybe feeling a little excluded by the others or maybe not, but falling behind nonetheless. Anya turned, called back to her friend, and waited while the girl trotted to catch up. It was a tiny thing, something anyone but a child's parents would be unlikely to notice, but it made my day.

Anya's version of nine is off to a start full of privilege, opportunity, and easy good times, for which I am profoundly grateful. By American and British financial standards, we're barely middle class. But I've got a fantastic job that's paying for us to be in Scotland, and that lets Amy and me spend money on our daughter as only a tiny percentage of this world's parents can.

These living daydreams, though, grateful as I am for them, don't even come close to what I most want to give my daughter. What I most want to give her—and what I'm determined she must never confuse for trips or horse lessons—is, of course and simply, love.

That spiritually essential feeling that her parents love her, without reservation or complication, wholly and forever.

Love in childhood teaches you that you belong in this world, for the rest of your life. It opens you to compassion and trust and new loves of your own. Our young family friend Briana, the daughter of the minister who fifteen summers ago married Amy and me, has come to visit from America. She's a favorite of Anya's, and she brought her a birthday gift, a fisherman's style cap she's been working on making for months. In the cottage kitchen, she played "Happy Birthday" on fiddle while Amy and I sang. Anya blew out the candles on her cake, on which I'd spent an hour drawing a colored-frosting fox.

The kind of love my mother showed me is infinitely harder to measure than stuffed toys or fancy hot chocolate or even handmade hats and hand-decorated cakes. And infinitely more valuable. And it's the one gift I am most determined to give Anya.

Less than a month left to live here. It's good to mourn your life a little as you lead it. You notice more. The cobbled backstreets of St. Andrews grow narrow and ancient again, with iron lampposts angling out from stone walls. The stones of Crail's seawall are once again speckled with silver and orange lichen in the sun. Out the window beyond my desk the North Sea again becomes the North Sea, with dusk clouds darkening the Isle of May into the horizon.

I doubt that we will ever return to live in Crail. Certainly, we will never return to Anya newly nine, Amy forty, and the three of us living in the harbour cottage with the address the same as my age—"41"—in pewter on the red front door.

Numbered days.

But then, they are all numbered. Every life is leaving, never to return.

Look, I can hear my mom's voice urge. I can see her emerald-green eyes happily taking in her own numbered days. I can see the soft freckles around those green eyes.

Look.

Anya didn't want to wear a safety pin to keep her new kilt, which was a size too big, from sliding down. As she got ready for her Highland-dance class, she was adamant the kilt fit.

"Fine," I said. "You'll just be pulling it up again and again while you're trying to dance." I was tired and edgy from working on what is now my Keats and Fanny novel.

I glimpsed Anya's half-concerned, half-hurt expression, but she recovered quickly enough to say, "Fine." And out the door we went.

I was quiet through the drive to St. Andrews as I tried to right my mood while Anya and Briana chatted in the back seat. Briana had watched Anya's riding lesson over the weekend, so the two of them were talking Barnsmuir Farm horses.

Anya said she hadn't seen Cinderella in the pasture lately.

"Maybe Alice moved her to another pasture, Sweetie," Amy offered. "Or . . . well, thirty-five is very old for a horse."

"Maybe she died?"

"Maybe so, Kiddo. We'll ask Alice next time."

"What would she have died *from*?"

Amy answered just old age, but Anya wanted to know how. What specifically about old age would make her die?

"The organs just get worn out and stop working," I offered.

"Maybe kidney failure," Briana clarified. She'd spent much of her senior year of high school working in a vet clinic. "The kidneys filter out the toxins from the blood," she continued. "When they stop working, the toxins build up in your blood and poison you. Poison your brain actually. It's a painful way to go."

I didn't recall any pain, I objected silently.

Well, there was lots of pain, as there had been for a long time. But not from the kidney failure.

And that fast I was back in the last week of my mother's life; the great care not to touch her purple hands and her finger stubs when we moved her from her wheelchair to bed; the little pink lollipop sponge dabbed on her lips and on which she sucked to sooth the thrush in her mouth; the delicate swabbing of her soiled backside where patches of skin had come away from the flesh and all those invisible nerves.

My father and sister and I sang "Under the Boardwalk" as we cleaned her.

"Sounds good," my mom managed to say through her winces. Two of maybe twelve words she'd managed all day.

The verse about the blanket by the sea—*where I'll be*—couldn't come back around fast enough.

"That's what happens with animals. It's different with people, though," Briana went on as I slowed Pigeon into the cobbled streets of St. Andrews. "People get dialysis, a kidney machine they get hooked up to while they wait for a transplant."

"Nana got that, Baby," Amy said. "Do you remember visiting her at dialysis?"

Three times a week, every week, she sat in the big recliner. Often she graded freshman-composition papers for my dad. The stack of papers and a rubber-banded bundle of yellow plastic mechanical pencils sat atop the humming contraption tethered by her side, at least until the erosion of her fingers made writing comments on the papers too painful. Amy and Anya and I would drop by to visit and bring our descriptions of the weather outside. Every once in a while, when it was warm and sunny and my mom had the strength, she'd suggest we all go for a drive down to the lake when her dialysis was done and maybe stop along the way and get a "little something" at Frosty Treats.

"Yeah!" Anya would agree, and I'd catch the smiling looks from other patients and nurses and technicians.

"Did Nana get a transplant?" Anya asked as I turned at a little roundabout.

"No. Daddy was going to give her a kidney."

"But then Daddy would need dialysis," Anya said with sudden concern.

"You only need one kidney," Amy explained. "Everyone has two."

"But you didn't give her one?"

We passed slowly between the elm trees lining the street.

"She was never well enough to have surgery," I explained. "You can't have any open wounds."

This had been explained to my mom, dad, sister, and me as we sat around a table in a small windowless consultation room in the University of Wisconsin hospital. Dad, Ann, and I had taken blood tests. The cheery surgeon's assistant had just told us my dad was off the hook and so was my sister but, great news, I was a match! Now we sat with the surgeon, who told us that only 20 percent of people on dialysis are still alive after five years without a transplant.

Somehow, I had imagined we might go on forever. I had imagined that we could continue as we had, helping my mom slide from the dialysis-unit recliner to her wheelchair and heading out for our drives down to the lake. Sometimes, Anya and Amy and I would play on the playground equipment, and my mom would watch and cheer and wave. Though I felt to my core the family imperative to value every moment of some limited number of days we would not get back, I had simultaneously permitted myself to imagine that dialysis could keep those days coming indefinitely.

But 80 percent of people gone in five years . . .

I'd never seen a human being so clean, groomed, and wholly right in the world as that surgeon. Sitting at that table with him, my family seemed small and fragile. My mom seemed small and fragile.

Beside the exit out of the transplant center at the UW hospital, there was a wall of dark-blue glass into which the names of living organ donors were etched in white. The wall was backlit so the donors' names glowed.

Go home and heal the last little open wound on your leg stump, my mom was told. "We'll go from there."

We'll go from there. A favorite phrase among those in the medical fields.

Where we went from there was the student union on the UW campus. What better place could there be for my family to go to feel secure and home again? We brought our trays outside to the tables next to Lake Mendota. At how many student union tables on how many campuses had we made ourselves at home? I remember the folk singers in the sun at the University of Utah. This same family, young and strong, my father wearing a plaid cotton shirt my mother had made.

I don't recall what we spoke about at the UW union, but it wasn't open wounds or kidneys. We were alive together in the sun, students and professors passing around us, my mother's wheelchair turned so she could see the sailboats on the little lake.

Later, though, beside Lake Superior, alone with Amy, I did talk about wounds. And she and I talked about kidneys, my mother's and mine. We stood on the sand in the dark and watched the lighthouse beam sweep over the water, and I told her I wanted to do it, wanted to give my mom a kidney.

My mom had resolved not to let me. Even before we'd gone down to Madison for the consultation, she'd said she wouldn't take an organ from one of her children. Before putting you on a donor waiting list, the transplant team wants to test members of your family for a match, so she'd gone along with that much. But just to get on the waiting list. Or in case Dad was a match, but even then she wasn't certain.

But it was me.

I explained to Amy about the donor's six-week recovery and the expectation of a totally normal life after that. A totally normal life with my mom—Anya's Nana, Amy's dear friend—still around where otherwise she would likely not be. The list for strangers' kidneys is notoriously long, and the rejection rate is far higher than with family members' kidneys.

Amy agreed with my prediction that my mom would remain steadfastly against it. She'd do nothing to put me—her son, Anya's father—at even the smallest risk.

I told Amy I had time to work on convincing my mom. What a chance she'd be giving me. A chance to do something better and more generous than I'd ever imagined possible. I'd tell her I could think of no place in the world I'd rather see my name than on that blue-glass wall. Amy and I both knew that right then, with the sound of Superior's little waves sloshing on the sand, I was working on convincing her too.

But there was no timeline, no way of knowing when all of this might come to pass, if ever. The wound on my mother's leg stump had been open for months. For years, more often than not she had been nursing one or another open wound. The stump would most likely heal, we'd been told, but when was anyone's guess.

So we'd wait and we'd see. We'd go from there. Me and my mom, each sure what we'd do for the other.

It was my mom who won, of course. I sit in the garden now, overlooking the North Sea, writing this with both kidneys inside me, just as my mom put me into the world. There was never a time, for the rest of her life, when every wound was healed.

Which means we sort of had it both ways, I suppose. For the rest of her life, I got to be the son waiting to give her this extraordinary gift, and she knew she'd refuse me.

From the back seat of Pigeon, Anya asked why you can't get a new kidney when you have open wounds. Briana explained about the drugs they have to give you to suppress your immune system and how those drugs increased your risk of infection.

"Besides," I added, "Nana wouldn't let me."

"How come?"

"She didn't want her child to have an operation like that." My voice was rock steady. These were the facts I'd known I'd one day tell her, and I was relieved that I could tell them straight.

"She didn't want you to have surgery if you didn't have to?"

"That's right. But I wanted to," I said. I explained there never came a time when she didn't have at least one open wound.

Soon, Briana, Amy, and I were sitting along the wall of the dance studio with other parents and friends watching our kilted children turn circles and swing their pointed toes and hold their small hands up, thumbs touching middle fingers, other fingers raised like the antlers of Highland stags.

A children's dance class. How simple. How common. How miraculous to be there. How tentative and temporary.

Afterward, as we walked back to the car, I told Anya I was sorry I'd given her grief about not using a safety pin to cinch up her kilt. I was glad it hadn't seemed to bother her.

"I didn't even notice," she said.

And then, because there we were, alive at the same place and in the same moment, I could say to my child, "Well, you danced wonderfully!"

A discovery.

I have been staying up late writing while out the window off the end of my desk, the May's lighthouse keeps time in the endless blue dusk. Poems come in over the inky water and find me in the little yellow light of my lamp. Last night though, for as long as I stared out where that island breached the horizon and flashed, no lines came. For some distraction I finally took out the folder my aunt Charleen had sent me. In it was everything she had been able to gather of our family history on my mom's side.

Everyone was from Scotland, that much I'd always known. My mother's Nana had spoken some Gaelic now and then. As a boy, my uncle was taught to dance a Highland fling. Based on these clues I have always chosen to believe at least some of my ancestors came from the Highlands.

Where exactly was another matter. As I paged through the file, I opened my laptop and searched dozens of names and dates, but no places turned up.

I flipped more pages until I came to a copy of a document with the promising title "Family Tree." Like leaves on the tree, in neat cursive, were names . . . and birthplaces! Vancouver, Canada. Inverness, Scotland. And my great-great-grandparents, John MacLure and Ann Campbell MacLure, were both born in a place called Glenelg.

I'd heard the name before or seen it on a sign or map somewhere.

I typed in the name of the place, clicked Search Maps, and there it was. Yes, in the Highlands! A tiny village on the mountainous coast looking across a narrow strait of sea to the Isle of Skye. Glenelg. Just twenty-five linear miles from Loch Shiel, the first place in Scotland I'd gone to speak to my mother and to listen for her voice.

Now I had found another place, a place where I might go and say to my mother, *Here they lived who led to us.* A place I might take Anya and say to her, *Here they lived who led to you.*

Glenelg. That would do for one night. I turned off the light and clicked closed the laptop. Out the window the sea and sky were finally, at one in the morning, almost dark. Almost, but not quite. The next day was already beginning.

❦

If our own heritage is the past, someone else's heritage is now. And so I offer them this scene: Amy, Anya, and I sit beside a fire down the beach from our cottage. With us are friends from Scotland and friends from home, including Briana. She stands barefoot out on the rock reef exposed by low tide and plays her fiddle under the longest dusk of the year. Our other American friends are teaching our Scottish friends to make s'mores. The graham crackers, Hershey's chocolate bars, and the big marshmallows everyone takes turns roasting on sticks have come across the Atlantic Ocean in suitcases.

If somehow you are reading this, descendent of mine, the fiddle music over the water was slow and sweet. The fire was little. It crackled and popped with its small warmth, and Anya, my child, sat snug in my arms and was the answer to everything.

Marquette, Day Six Continues

February 7, afternoon . . .

I told her I cleaned the house. I made Ann's bed.

She made a breath of "Yes."

She said, "Help me."

I said, "We will, yes. We'll help you. I'll help you."

We sat her up farther.

Mozart's Requiem *played.*

The sun, the actual sun *came through the window for about thirty seconds, and I told her about that.*

I told her Ann was going to take a shower, to get her face ready for the faces she'll meet—a variation on an Eliot quote she's always delighted using.

She breathed, "Yes," again.

Dad was out in the living room for a little while.

She kept working to keep her eyes open.

I told her she could go be with the geese.

I told her, Let's go on living ten years ago. Let's keep on walking around the island, the four of us. Let's live there always.

She opened her eyes, struggling, and said, "I love you."

I said, "I love you, Mom. We all love you."

She breathed once, twice more, opened her mouth.

I called Dad. He came in.

I said, "Go get Ann."

He did.

Ann came in. We all said, "We're here. It's OK."

Aunt Charleen and Uncle Ron came in. She was still there. I am certain. They told her they were here.

Charleen said, "Go and be with Nana and Mom and Dad."

Later, Rick came in to be alone with her. Amy came in to be alone with her. Others she loved.

Before, when it was happening and I was alone with her, I held her and held her and Mozart's Requiem *played, and she said, "I love you," and I told her again and again and again, "You did a good job."*

Before that, before Ann left for her shower, I told her, "You made everything bright. You made every day bright and wonderful."

Scotland, Midsummer

I HAVE NEVER put much stock in the notion of genetic memory, but one look at Glenelg and I began to wonder. Amy, Anya, and I drove a single-lane road up switchbacks climbing through evergreen forest so steep Pigeon's motor strained, even in low gear, until we came to the top of Ratagan Pass. There, spread out below us, was the place for which I suddenly knew I'd always been searching. The mountains *and* the sea. Rocky peaks rimmed the glen's long parabolic slopes of open moorland and heather and more evergreen forests, all curving down to square and rectangle pastures and stands of deciduous trees spread along the silver-blue of a river winding down to the blue coast. A place I'd never seen before. A place I recognized instantly.

"Daddy?" Anya asked. "Do you think I could pick some flowers, in case we find the graves?"

We pulled off by the "Welcome to Glenelg" sign, where Anya selected one stem of blossoms from a patch of wild purple foxgloves. We drove on, over a cattle grate and down the narrow road that descended past farms and pastures and mossy stacked-stone fences. Soon we came to a little cemetery on the valley floor. If they had been born here, perhaps they were buried here.

As we stepped through the gate I suggested we spread out. We'd only just begun to search when Amy said, "Over here."

There, under the reach of an elm's branches, was a silvery-gray marble headstone with the names John MacLure and Ann

Campbell chiseled in white lettering. My great-great-grandparents. Born and, indeed, buried here. Surrounding them were other MacLure headstones, a whole group of them.

Anya laid her single stem of purple flowers. Amy took photos. I stood there quietly, letting the reality of what we had found rise and fill the air around us.

Every MacLure headstone had a symbol, an interlocking *M*, *C*, and *L*. Each was also inscribed with the same Gaelic words, "Gus am bris an lá." The big elms shaded the headstones while sun shone across nearby pastureland and up the greenest slopes imaginable. All my life I have sought places as one way of making sense of my life. Now I had this one. And this place had me. It had been waiting.

We drove the rest of the way into the tiny village, past the village hall and little primary school, stopping a couple times for sheep in the road. We bought ice cream cones at the whitewashed Glenelg Store and sat on a bench outside eating them. Beside us hung baskets of flowers Amy said my mom would have liked.

"Yes," I agreed. "She'd have liked everything here." It occurred to me that this place had been here all along and she died without knowing. I could never even tell her about it. That injustice dimmed the brilliance of our new discovery a little.

But would I have come here if she hadn't died?

An earthy woman with long curly gray hair passed us with "Lovely day."

"Summer's here," Amy replied.

"Aye, long may it last."

I asked if she might happen to know of any living MacLures in the area.

"You'll want to talk to Uisdean," she said. "Uisdean and Christina. At Riverfoot." She pointed across a delta of pasture at a cottage backdropped by the sea.

"Are they MacLures?" Anya asked.

"Aye, MacLures. And he knows the history of the glen well as anyone."

The possibility that I might have some living connection to this place was almost too wondrous to consider. As soon as that possibility presented itself, though, came the fear that I might not. I wasn't ready to find out. I needed time to steady myself.

We drove through the tiny heart of the village and found an older cemetery in the yard of a small white church right on the shore. Here were *more* MacLures. Dates back into the eighteenth century. Dates obscured by wind and rain's erosion.

And again on the MacLure stones, the words "Gus am bris an lá." Could it be we had a family motto? Could it be that there was a "we"?

Amy, Anya, and I had been close to this place before, twenty-five linear miles south at Loch Shiel. We'd driven right by the turnoff to Ratagan Pass and the glen on our way to visit a castle with Amy's parents last fall. Across a narrow sound of sea from the older Glenelg cemetery rose the mountains of the Isle of Skye. We'd been there too. It was as though something in me had been homing, circling this place, seeking it all year. And before then, too, when we'd chosen Scotland for our year abroad. And my whole life, when I've been drawn—as I have since childhood—to hidden-away mountainscapes. To remote coasts.

I was still hesitant when at last we drove from the old cemetery out onto the delta of land where the river meets the sea, to Riverfoot, the cottage of Uisdean and Christina. It had begun to occur to me that my connection with anyone living here might be unclear or completely unknowable. If I wasn't ready for answers, neither was I ready for ambiguity, though ambiguity seemed a likely—perhaps the most likely—outcome.

The name on the mailbox was MacLure, but there was nobody home. I was disappointed, but was I also a little relieved? I left a note explaining who I was, the American great-great-grandson of John MacLure and Ann Campbell MacLure in the cemetery. I'd be in Scotland three more weeks, I wrote, and left our Crail address and phone number.

So perhaps we'd never know. At least not now. I could live with that. I had found this place. My ancestral home. And my mother's. And Anya's.

We pulled back onto the road, heading down the shore toward a beach to gather some shells to send to my aunt Charleen in thanks for the old family papers that had led us here. An elderly woman was pushing a small child in a stroller—a pram, as the Scots say—down the road. I pulled alongside her and rolled down my window.

"Pardon me. I'm a MacLure on my mother's side, and I'm looking for any MacLures in the village." I explained that we'd been directed to Uisdean and Christina, but there was nobody home at Riverfoot Cottage.

"Ah, well then. Their daughter Catherine lives on the farm you would have passed on your way down into the glen. Lamont's her married name." She looked at her wristwatch. "But she'll be at the school just now, picking up her children."

"Children?"

"Yesss!" Anya whispered from the back seat.

"Aye. But she should be back home soon enough. You should stop there."

I thanked her and asked, "Just one more thing. Do the MacLures go back in Glenelg a long time?"

She looked at me over the top of her glasses. "Aye. Thirteenth century."

I felt something like a wind move through me. The breaths of eight hundred years of people. My mother's people. In this place she never knew. That I almost never knew.

We walked the beach—the beach of my ancestors—and collected our shells.

"I love it here," Anya said. "It's like the picture I drew for you of the house to look for, Daddy."

Indeed it was. We'd passed several cottages by the sea like Riverfoot, like the one I'd found for us in Crail. But behind these cottages, mountains rose straight up, like in the picture of hers I'd brought with me when I'd come house hunting alone a year ago. The picture below which she'd written "Good by Dady!! I love you!! Git a good house!!"

"I'm glad we came to Crail, though," she said. "I love it there and the cottage you found. I just mean, Glenelg is, you know . . ."

"Yeah, I know."

On our way back up the road toward Ratagan Pass, we pulled off at the farm of Catherine Lamont. I got out and knocked on the door, but nobody answered here either.

"Nobody's home?" Anya asked dejectedly.

"I'm sorry." I was about to write another note explaining who I was when I spotted a girl about ten climbing over a gate just down the road. I walked over and asked if she might happen to know a Catherine Lamont.

"She's just in there," the girl said and pointed to a barn from which an electric motor was buzzing.

I called Amy and Anya from the car, and the three of us crossed the farmyard and passed a pair of Shetland ponies and some more kids playing with a couple of puppies. We looked through the barn door and saw a woman and three men shearing sheep.

"Pardon me," I shouted over the rattle of the shears.

They all looked up from their work. The shears stopped.

"Are you Catherine Lamont?"

"Yes."

I apologized for the interruption and introduced myself.

"I think we might be related."

Catherine led us back outside. She was a few years younger than me. Her blond hair was pulled back in a ponytail. The sun shone on the freckles on her arms and face. It was my mother's skin.

I introduced Amy and Anya.

There was kindness in Catherine's eyes as she studied me. "So you're a MacLure?"

"The graves in the cemetery. John MacLure and Ann Campbell. I think they were my great-great-grandparents."

"Really? I don't know as much about the family history as my dad. He's the one you should talk to. How long are you in Glenelg?"

"We have to leave soon," I said. We had a dinner invitation a long drive from here.

"He and Mum are away to Inverness. It'd be good if you could talk to him."

The girl I'd spotted climbing over the fence arrived with a package in her hands, clearly a pitchfork. Each tine was individually—as though for a joke—wrapped in shipping paper. It looked like a papier-mâché pitchfork. Everything here was marvelous.

"Mum, it came."

Catherine introduced the girl as her daughter Megan. She called her other three children over from the puppies. The girl she introduced as Caitlin. She was about Anya's age. The little boys, she said, were Campbell and Callum.

I introduced myself and Amy and Anya. The kids all shook hands politely.

Megan commenced unwrapping her new pitchfork, but otherwise the children stood by, inspecting these strangers with American accents.

"Well," Catherine said with a smile. "Come in the house a while won't you? Anya, would you like to stay and help this lot wash down the ponies?"

"Yes, please!"

"Can you guys show Anya what to do?"

Those kind eyes, with the rising slopes of the glen behind and the clear sky above, were not the exact green of my mother's. But they were as close as any I'd ever seen.

"Ah," she exclaimed as she gazed up at the sound of a car slowing in the road. "There's Mum and Dad now."

The car stopped alongside the gate. The window rolled down, and Megan, Caitlin, Campbell, and Callum ran over and greeted their grandparents.

"Perfect timing," Catherine said. "Come on. I'll introduce you."

Uisdean had an old man's good looks, with bright-blue eyes that reminded me of Paul Newman's, a shock of thick white hair, and that familiar fair skin, weathered in his case from decades working outside. Christina beside him also had short white hair and bright, beautiful eyes too. She nodded politely.

As they sat in the idling car, Catherine leaned down and explained that we were in Glenelg researching our ancestors.

"We've had a bit of a drive just now," Christina said apologetically. "How long are you in Glenelg?"

"They've got to be away soon, Mum. Just pull up to the house for a minute."

Catherine stood up and paid us a wink over the roof of the car.

Uisdean drove the car to the driveway, and Catherine said, "So Anya, you want to help with the ponies? You kids take care of her, she's probably your relative!"

I grabbed my family-history file from the car, and we followed Catherine inside. She apologized for the clutter in the kitchen and explained that they were just getting ready to build a new house. I didn't tell her how at home I felt in an old farm kitchen with stacks of canned food and piles of work gloves on the counter.

She poured us juices in Winnie-the-Pooh glasses—Tigger for Amy, Piglet for me—and we sat down at the table with her parents.

I explained that we'd come to Glenelg looking for John MacLure and Ann Campbell's graves and found them among all the other MacLures in the cemetery.

"He's up in the old cemetery," Uisdean said. Of course he would be, I realized. He'd died in 1901. We must have missed him there. The headstone with both their names in the new cemetery must mark just Ann's grave.

"We did go to the old cemetery," I said and told him we'd found lots of MacLures.

He said a man came through here one time doing research. The man had thought that way back MacLures were Dewers, that they came from Ireland through Perth. The name probably became MacDewer, son of Dewer.

"And that became MacLure?" I asked.

"Aye."

"And they've been here since the thirteenth century?"

He gave a half nod, half shrug. Was he seventy or maybe even eighty? Handsome, lean, and sinewy as he was, it was hard to say.

"There was something written on the graves. Gaelic, I think."

"Gus am bris an lá," Uisdean said. "Until the day breaks."

He said something else in Gaelic to Christina.

"Till the day break, or until the day breaks," she said.

I took a copy of the family tree out of the file and slid it across the table. I pointed out my mother's father, Iain MacLure, and his father Donald, born in Inverness, son of John MacLure and Ann Campbell, both born in Glenelg.

"My grandparents," he said.

"Your grandparents?"

"That's Don my uncle. There was two Dons went to Vancouver. My dad's brothers."

"Both Don?"

"Aye." He and Christina exchanged a few more words in Gaelic.

"Big Don and Little Don," Christina said. "They started a taxi company."

"The older one went on to California," Uisdean said. His pronunciation of "Cal-ee-forn-ya" made the place of my mother's birth and my birth seem far away and exotic.

"There was one that worked in Hollywood."

"Hollywood?" I puzzled a moment. "Oh yes, he worked on glass!"

"Aye."

"He made windows and glass eyes for monsters and things. For Warner Brothers. That was Don's son Iain. My grandfather."

Uisdean nodded and repeated, "In California."

"Yes. So, your grandfather is my great-great-grandfather?"

"Aye. We lost touch with them in California some years ago."

"My mother's parents died young, in 1962."

"Ah, right," he said. Just "Ah, right." As if to say, *That explains that then*, as the half-century mystery of lost relations was cleared up.

"This is so interesting," Catherine said. "Tell about your trip to Vancouver, Dad."

Uisdean said they'd been over some years back to visit the MacLures there.

"They sold the taxi service, but it's still called MacLure Taxis," Christina added.

We went through the relationships again until we had it solid in our minds: Uisdean's grandparents, John and Ann, were my great-great-grandparents; his father was brother to my great-grandfather; my grandfather and Uisdean were cousins, which made Catherine and me cousins, and Anya and Catherine's kids outside cousins.

"Amazing," Catherine said.

We all sat back with the satisfaction of something accomplished, though unsure quite what. This was an experience entirely unlike any I'd ever had.

What did they make of us? Me with my beard, shaggy hair, and eager questions. Amy with her smile over at me, pleased by the obvious joy I was taking in this. Catherine said we should organize a MacLure reunion in the States and they'd all come over. And she offered for us to bunk down in the little wooden chalets they rent out to hill walkers, if we could come back and stay some time. I remembered passing those chalets beyond the dry-stone fence beside the road on the way into Glenelg. Those chalets, a couple stables, the barn, and this farmhouse. Just another lovely pastoral cluster of buildings, for all I'd known.

I finished my juice from the Piglet glass, and Christina said they really did have to be getting home, but they hoped to see us again. I told them about the note I'd left at their house and that it had all our contact details. Catherine and I exchanged addresses.

Outside Amy took a picture of Uisdean and me standing beside his car, both of us with crooked, satisfied, only slightly uncomfortable smiles. I shook his hand, which was as lean and weathered as the rest of him, but his grip was gentle. I promised to return for a proper visit.

"Aye, good. Yes," he said. Christina paid us a smile and wave as they backed out, and then they were gone.

As Catherine, Amy, and I strolled back to the barnyard, Catherine said she was so glad I'd come and wondered at our perfect timing to be there just as her parents drove by.

The other three men were done shearing for the day and leaned on the workbench chatting softly. They stood up straight as we walked in. Catherine introduced "the red-faced one" as her husband, Donnie. He was a young, handsome guy, all muscle in his sweaty tee shirt, dirty jeans, and buzz-cut hair. His handshake was firm and friendly.

"And his brother Ron. And Skip, here working from Australia."

Catherine told them we were her long-lost relatives from America. They nodded approvingly. I told them I was sorry for pulling Catherine away from the work.

"Don't be!" she said.

"She'll take any excuse," Donnie said and they all chuckled.

Catherine's kids and Anya wandered in while we talked.

"Do you want to meet the ponies?" Anya asked Amy and me.

We told the men thanks for sparing Catherine and it was lovely to meet them. Anya took Caitlin's hand as the children led Amy, Catherine, and me out to the paddock.

"I rode!" Anya said.

"I led," Megan reassured us. "Just around here."

"That's OK," Amy said.

The pair of Shetland ponies stood no taller than Anya herself.

Two of the fuzzy black-and-white border collie pups came bounding over. Anya and little Campbell picked up a squirming one each.

Amy took pictures of the kids with the animals while Catherine and I stood there, shielding our eyes from the sun with our hands. A few blond locks had come loose from where she'd tied her hair back to work.

"This is an amazing place," I said, glancing up at the hills rising around us.

She looked around with me and put her hands on her hips. "We like it here. What is it you do in the States?"

I told her I was a professor and a poet.

"A poet?"

"Mostly. Along with other writing here and there."

"Cousins," she said simply.

"You look like my mom," I offered. "Your complexion. Your freckles."

"Oh," she smiled and looked at the back of her arm.

"And your nose. And your eyes are green, like hers."

For a moment I found myself unable to speak.

Amy lined up the kids and Catherine and me for more photos, then we said we should push on. Catherine and I agreed to exchange written versions of our family-branch histories in the mail.

"I'll get all I can from Dad," she said. "But we will see you again, I hope."

I promised we'd return. And looking up into the hills a last time, I knew just how much I meant it. I would walk the trails up there, where someone in my place would have walked had my great-grandfather Don stayed home. I would walk there and speak into the air, to what would have been. I would sleep and wake and sleep again in this glen. And I would get to know Catherine better, and her sister, whom she said lives just a few villages up the coast, and their brother who's still in Glenelg. I would bring Anya so she'd get to know better her Scottish cousins. I would see to it that what was restored, this legacy my mother unknowingly gave us, will go on.

Catherine and her kids waved at the gate as we drove up the road out of Glenelg. As Pigeon revved into the steep ascent I looked out over the valley headlands.

The mountains curving around the top of the glen reminded me of places I love in Idaho and Montana, and the rugged, remote coast below made me think of upper Michigan. Places where I've known exquisite belonging and to which I've felt a draw so powerful at times it's seemed the most important thing in my life to get back to.

In a way I guess it matters if there has always been some deep genetic or perhaps even spiritual memory drawing me to Glenelg. In the same way I guess it matters if the sentient spirits of this place—and even of my mother—led me here and can lead me still, through the rest of my days. In another way, though, it doesn't matter at all. Either way those who came before give us what they are, their places, and their loves, and then they go. And what they have given us stays. Even when their names are lost to us, are faded from stone. Even when their ashes, like my mother's, are scattered to distant waters. Who they were can lead us, if we only follow ourselves.

We would be back with the MacLures in Glenelg someday. I promised myself. But before we left the Highlands for who knew how many years, we had one more thing to do. We had a train to catch.

The Hogwarts Express is how we and hundreds of millions of kids and their parents around the world have come to know it, but the antique steam train from Fort William to Mallaig is officially called the Jacobite. We boarded at the Fort William station, and from the moment Amy opened the old wood-and-glass door to what was an exact match to the train compartment in the films and said Hermione's words, "Come on, everywhere else is full," we were inside Anya's dream. For two hours as the train chugged its steam-and-smoke-trailing way beside lochs and through mountains and over the famous viaduct overlooking Loch Shiel, we played.

Wordsworth says the world we perceive is one we also half create. That belief was a kind of gospel my mom passed on to me. Just as she never saw Glenelg or knew her relatives living there, my mom never read so much as a page of the Harry Potter books. Our family enthrallment with that world didn't begin until shortly after she had gone. But there was no doubt in my mind as I watched

Anya look out the window over her Nana's near namesake loch, searching for Hogwarts Castle on one of those seemingly empty, far peninsulas, that one way or another, my mother had led us here too.

"See it yet, Harry?" I asked.

"It's there, Ron."

The end draws closer. For her final show-and-tell of the school year, Anya wants to talk about Glenelg and her cousins with their Shetland ponies there. I draw a family tree showing her connection to her Scottish relations.

"Perfect," she says.

We have long, lingering dinners with Scotland friends. One evening Alan, Debbie, and Callum visit. In front of our cottage the adults eat smoked mackerel, and the kids make short work of French toast and run down to the beach to build a sandcastle.

We made a life here, a life we've come to love and feel at home in, and that life will soon be over. We'll let it go fondly, but as gracefully as we can.

Good practice, I guess.

Later, while Amy and Anya sleep, I walk outside and leave the door open behind me. In bare feet I make my way around the harbour and up the stone steps onto the seawall. I turn and look back at the dark windows of the cottage under a sky that at eleven thirty at night still looks like dusk on a stage set. The harbour lights reflect in the inkwell harbour where boats are tethered by sagging ropes. When I turn and look out to sea, the low, lingering haar obscures the Isle of May, but the lighthouse manages to pulse its location amber through the fog. Above, just a few stars show in the indigo sky.

Today Woody has pink and purple ribbon braided on the brow-band under his white forelocks. He's a little girl's dream of a pony. The sweetest month on a little girl's calendar of ponies. The pony a little girl would invite for tea in the rose garden.

I know better. I've seen him running flat out with my daughter screaming on his back for her mother, his white mane fluttering like a banner behind his hell-bent head.

Alice hasn't asked Anya if she wants to ride Woody again since the day he spooked and she got back on him briefly to prove to herself she could. But inside the cool air of the stone barn, while Anya buckles and adjusts her padded riding hat, Alice asks her if she fancies a go on Patch or Woody today.

Patch has become Anya's usual, her steady buddy. Old reliable Patch. For my money, they've been just right for each other. And at first Anya says she'll ride him.

"No, Woody."

"All right," Alice says.

"No wait, Patch."

"OK."

"No wait, what are we going to do?"

"We can do a ride out or work in the paddock."

Anya thinks for a moment more.

"Woody. In the paddock," she says definitively.

"Well done, you," Alice says.

And I do what is often the hardest thing any parent can do, keep silent.

And so she rides Woody. It's an individual lesson, just Alice and Anya. No jumps, nothing fancy. Alice is right there watching every move, her proper English voice guiding both horse and girl. But even so, Anya rides Woody.

Amy and I stand at the fence. My breaths move thick and slow in and out of my tight chest. She looks good out there, we agree as we watch her confident, rising trots around a circuit of orange cones. The sun shines. House martins whistle and chatter in the rows of enormous maple trees and swoop low over the grass. In the adjoining field a crop sprinkler shoots its long, arcing streams of spray.

"You're in charge, Anya," Alice assures her. "Good! Well done."

Then a hollow hiss comes from somewhere. From the Underworld itself. Then a few miles offshore the specks of two jet fighters approach low.

Anya brings Woody to a stop.

The specks grow into shapes as they get closer and louder. They're going to pass right overhead. There's no time for help. Anya holds the reigns taut. The jets cut the air like huge scalpels. The scream of them drowns out the birds and thought.

But Woody stands.

They thunder over and crackle away.

Woody stands.

The birdsong returns.

"Trot on," Anya says with authority. And Woody does.

Last things.

Amy takes some final photos of the narrow lanes and whitewashed cottages, of the bright fishing boats floating in the harbour, of low sunlight on the green Isle of May. More than twenty-five thousand times this year, she's raised the camera to her eye and made an image of what she's seen. My favorite is still a picture from our first weeks—Anya seen from behind, facing the sea. She is standing barefoot on the rocks, wearing red-plaid pants and a white tee shirt. The breeze lifts her hair up and out above her shoulders. Blue sky and clouds reflect in the rock pools, and turquoise waves lift from the cobalt water. When I look at that picture the whole year is ahead of us.

Up in St. Andrews, at a café where I've written from time to time, I bring the staff an armful of roses from our cottage garden. Bringing flowers to any café where I've written is a parting ritual I began in Marquette the summer after my mother died. I brought the staff at the Third Street Bagel Shop there a bouquet from her garden, a huge, raucous bunch of blossoms spraying out from the vase. They'd placed them on the counter, and I'd left Marquette thinking about the people of her town coming and going all day seeing and smelling her flowers.

I fly down to London; ride the tube out to Hampstead; emerge from the station into the center of the old village; wind my way down lanes lined with enormous beech, elm, and maple; and arrive at Wentworth Place. One house comprised of two attached residences. Keats's and Fanny Brawne's. Under a gray sky wind is bending the boughs of the trees in the garden around the neat, white, villa-style home. The real place where two real people fell in love. Where one of them wrote poems I've known almost as long as I can remember. The house is closed for some restoration, but that's OK. It's enough to stand looking in at that setting, my arms folded on top of the garden fence.

Twenty-one years ago in Rome I stood in the room in which Keats died. I looked out over the sunlit piazza and watched the fountain gurgle and pigeons flap down from the tiled roofs to peck about on the ground beside the flower vendors.

He never made it back here from Rome, where he had gone hoping the warm, dry air would cure his tuberculosis. He left Wentworth Place and Fanny knowing he was likely to die without ever seeing either again. He left in part so that he and she might live with some last hope of his recovery and return. But he also left so that he could end as he chose, looking at this garden and his girl's face a final time and walking freely away from the greatest happiness he'd ever known. That this Eden might stay forever as it was.

The dead are gone from this earth. For all my searching, I've come no closer to knowing where they may be. I refuse all false comforts. I could call and call like a lost child for the rest of my days and still my mother would not come to me.

And yet she is here. In what she left. In how I see and live.

Keats is nowhere inside the fence I overlook. He and the girl who slept behind those windows and strolled those small grounds are utterly nonexistent. But he is here. Because I have come, he is here, in how I see and live.

The sky begins to sprinkle. I feel the rain a while before I open my umbrella and begin my walk back toward the tube station.

Our afterlife is one another.

Anya's school year ends with a service at the Crail church. The parents file through the Kirkyard cemetery, past all those parents and schoolchildren who came before. Pastor Mike is waiting with kilt and smile to greet us at the big wooden doors. He asks about our year and seems genuinely pleased to hear how much we've enjoyed it. When the service begins he talks of helping a local ornithologist put ankle bands on redshanks in the Crail Harbour so their history of place might be known wherever they may be found.

"And it is my hope that wherever all of you may go," he says to the blue-and-white-uniformed children in the first rows of pews, "your time at Crail School and the lessons you've learned and friends you've made and memories you have will go with you like those birds' ankle bands, not visible on the outside, but traveling through life with you just the same."

Kids as migratory birds. Not bad, I think.

Along with several others from the primary 4 class, Anya's been asked to say two sentences, something she remembers from the year and how it made her feel. She's kept her sentences a surprise from Amy and me, and we haven't a clue what she'll say when she steps to the microphone.

"My favorite memory from this year," she begins, by way of a title. I notice she's dropped the r at the end of year. Not quite the accent of her schoolmates, but no longer the accent she came here with.

"My favorite memory from this year," she continues, "is going to school in Scotland. It makes me feel like I've done something good with my life."

And as she walks proudly back to her pew, I know how she feels.

I'm up in the garden, sitting in the near dark of midnight, looking over the little harbour and cove beach below, out toward the Isle of May lighthouse light. The moon is full. A cloud slices through it then moves on, and the moon's white light brightens again on the surface of the sea. A gull cries over the soft, constant pulse of an infinity of water pulsing across sand and rock. My last moon from this garden. Is this a little what it's like to be done with your life?

No. Down below me, closer than sea and seawall and harbour, is the tiled roof beneath which sleep the two people who make me me. We'll leave Scotland and this part of our lives together. God willing, I will watch other moonrises while they dream.

No matter how much ends when we go, we go together. That makes our leaving no kind of death at all.

And yet, sitting out here in the perfect breeze off the water, the end of life as we have lived it in Scotland does feel like a kind of gentle rehearsal. I have been so happy here. The happiest I have been since the death of my mother. And now I sit and look at the moon and listen to the water's eternal body, and I make myself ready to go.

Marquette, Farewell

February 7, evening . . .

Sun. The snow finally cleared, and the sky was blue, a long, low sunny winter evening. We left the house to take Aunt Charleen to some of Mom's favorite places. Along the beach of Lake Superior and out to the trees and rocky shore of Presque Isle.

Meg, an old friend of Mom's, was parked, looking out at the water to the horizon.

We told her. A couple hours ago.

Meg had known it was coming. She said, "I came here because Sheila is here."

Scotland, Farewell

Our bags are packed, and the cottage is clean. It looks like it did when we arrived. We've straightened the oil paintings and dusted their gilded frames, stripped the beds, washed the bathroom rugs, and gathered all those sea shells we won't be taking home from windowsills and end tables and counter tops and put them in a box. We've even left some kindling and a few logs in the bucket beside the clean-swept fireplace for the new renters. For their first cold night.

Always leave things at least a little bit better than you found them, my mom used to say.

Pigeon is parked out of town beside our friend Christopher Rush's cottage. Chris's six-year-old daughter, Jenny, will ride in the middle of the back seat now. I couldn't be happier with the car's new owners—a writer and his family. It's a good car. I bet it runs for them another ten years just as safely and reliably as it did for us.

Life goes on, as it should.

Our suitcases are lined up down by the pier. Our ride to the airport will be here soon to collect us. We're ready ahead of schedule, a first in the history of our moves.

We take the box of shells back down to the beach from which they came and dump them rattling and softly clattering below the line of seaweed at the high-tide mark.

Anya's eyes water.

"Sad, Baby?" Amy asks.

She nods.

I search for my mother's wisdom and find it.

"Those shells are like our days here," I tell Anya. "We gathered them and enjoyed them and now we let them go."

"It's hard," she says as Amy and I each wrap an arm around her from either side.

"I know," I say. "That's because we've done a good job. We've been happy."

"We're very proud of you, Anya," Amy adds.

"I didn't want to come for a whole year."

"I remember," I tell her with a smile.

"Now I'm half and half," she says, looking at the sea. "I want to go. But I don't." Tears roll down her cheeks.

"That's me, too," Amy says.

"Thank you both, for the life we've had here," I say.

We write "Good-bye Crail" and our names in the sand beside the pile of dry white shells.

Anya wants to spend our last few minutes up on her bed before we go. Of course. Of all the places here to which she could feel the strongest connection and want to leave least, I can think of none more perfect than her bed, the bed of all those Harry Potter stories, of our "goodnight, Harry; goodnight, Ron" tuck ins, her nest for all those slumbers while the lighthouse blinked through the dark out her window.

She and Amy start back up the beach, but before I turn to follow I look out again to the horizon where blue meets blue. With all the gratitude I have for what wisdom and grace I manage to find, and for the man I've become to my two loves walking toward the cottage hand in hand just once more, and for the spirit that led me here and leads me to whatever is next, I whisper to the sea, "Thank you, Mom."

Acknowledgments

My thanks to Karen Babine, Sara Preisig, Natalie Kusz, and (every time) Amy Howko, readers whose insights helped make these better, truer words; Scott Olsen and the staff at *Ascent*, in which the Paris section was published as "Those Were the Days"; Annie Martin, Rachel Ross, Emily Nowak, Ceylan Akturk, Carrie Teefey, Salvatore Borriello, and the staff at Wayne State University Press for giving this book the perfect home; and Eastern Washington University for the funding and liberty of a faculty sabbatical (one of the most beautiful words in the English language).

My thanks also for the following permissions: Dr. Leslie Spry, National Kidney Foundation, quote from "Stopping Dialysis at the End of Life" from the *New York Times*, September 18, 2009, reprinted with the permission of the author; Ted Kooser, excerpt from "Mother" from *Delights & Shadows*, copyright © 2004 by Ted Kooser, reprinted with the permission of The Permissions Company, Inc. on behalf of Copper Canyon Press, www.coppercanyonpress.org.

About the Author

Photo by Amy Howko

Jonathan Johnson's previous works include the poetry books *May Is an Island*; *Mastodon, 80% Complete*; and *In the Land We Imagined Ourselves*; the memoir *Hannah and the Mountain*; and the play *Ode*. His poems have been published widely in magazines, anthologized in *Best American Poetry*, and read on National Public Radio. He continues to migrate between his Lake Superior coastal hometown of Marquette, Michigan; his ancestral glen in the costal Scottish Highlands; and Eastern Washington University, where he is a professor in the MFA program.